THE
PROTEIN
COOKBOOK

THE
PROTEIN
COOKBOOK

HEATHER THOMAS

EBURY
PRESS

CONTENTS

MAIN MEALS

PROTEIN POWDER

DESSERTS & BAKING

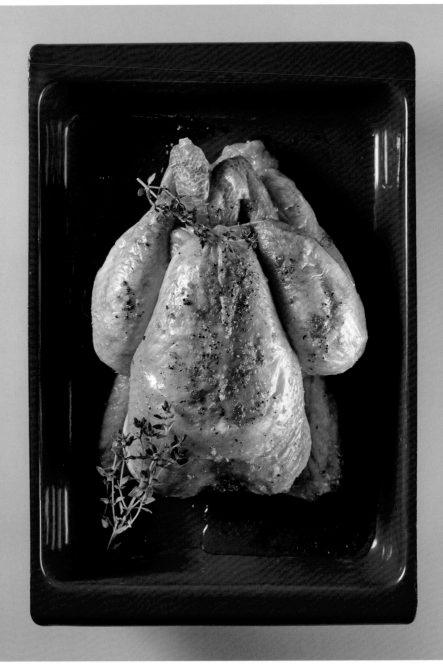

INTRODUCTION

Protein is essential for rebuilding, repairing and maintaining every cell in your body – from your internal organs, bones, muscles and blood to your skin, hair and nails. You can't live without protein; it helps to:

– Balance blood sugar levels.
– Improve insulin sensitivity and fight diabetes.
– Control and lower cholesterol and blood pressure.
– Build muscle mass and strength.
– Keep your immune system healthy.
– Prevent food cravings.
– Repair intestinal villi to aid absorption of nutrients.
– Boost your energy.

Protein is made up of organic compounds called amino acids; some of these are produced by your body, while the rest – the nine essential amino acids – are obtained from the food you eat. These are: histidine, isoleucine, leucine, lysine, methionine, phenylalanine, threonine, tryptophan and valine.

Animal and plant sources differ widely in which amino acids they provide, and although all nine are found in animal proteins (meat, poultry, fish and dairy foods), this is not the case with vegetable proteins (beans and pulses, nuts, seeds and grains), which means you need to eat them in different combinations.

HOW MUCH DO YOU NEED?

The amount of protein you need to support health, fitness and the repair of your body depends on your age, sex, weight and physical activity. The RDA (Recommended Dietary Allowance) for adults is a minimum of 0.8g protein per kilogram of body weight per day to stay healthy. That works out at approximately 55–60g (2–2½oz) per day for the average man and 45–50g (1½–2oz) for the average woman with a sedentary lifestyle.

To calculate how much protein you need per day, use this simple formula:

– Multiply your weight in pounds by 0.36, or multiply your weight in kilograms by 0.8.
– Double this figure if you are very active and exercise regularly.

Some people, including athletes, pregnant women, nursing mothers and people over 50 years old, have higher protein requirements (see below).

CAUTION: Consuming excessive amounts of protein over a period of time can be harmful to health. Current general guidelines suggest that you should not exceed 3.5g per kilogram of body weight but you should always consult your GP, or a qualified professional, to discuss your individual needs before changing your diet.

ATHLETES

If you're a professional athlete, work out regularly or exercise strenuously, you'll need additional protein to build and repair muscles, for energy and to recover from intense physical activity. For effective muscle growth it's important to eat a healthy diet and you may need twice as much protein as the average person – up to 2g protein per kilogram of body weight per day. If you don't get enough and are following a rigorous training schedule, you are more likely to feel fatigue and suffer from stress fractures and injuries that are slow to heal.

Even if you only exercise moderately, e.g. by walking briskly or stretching, you may need approximately 1g additional protein per kilogram of body weight.

Many athletes, especially those who do weight training, take protein supplements, and these can be useful in achieving your goals. We have included some recipes using protein powder in this book, but you can obtain all the protein you need by eating a healthy and varied diet, which contains plant proteins as well as (or in place of) animal ones.

PREGNANT WOMEN

When you're pregnant the quality and variety of the food you eat is so important to ensure you obtain all the nutrients that you and your baby need. Protein is important for the healthy development and growth of the baby, and to prepare your body for labour and breastfeeding. It is generally recommended that you should consume 1.5g protein per kilogram of weight per day, or between a minimum of 70g and a maximum of 100g, depending on your physical build and activity level. Nursing mothers also have a higher daily requirement for protein – at least 65g per day – to help them recover from labour and to promote their babies' healthy development and growth.

> **TIP:** If you're pregnant or lactating, talk to your doctor, midwife or nutritionist about your individual needs.

OLDER PEOPLE

After 50, and especially after 60, people start to lose muscle mass and their daily protein requirement will be higher. To maintain a healthy weight and strong muscles, and to protect your long-term cardiovascular health, you need to eat more protein-rich foods, especially lean protein, such as beans and pulses, eggs, oily fish and Greek yoghurt. Failure to do so can lead to muscle wastage and less strength, compromised mobility and balance, and taking longer to recover from injuries or illness.

So how much protein should you eat on a daily basis? International studies suggest that you consume 1.2g protein per kilogram of body weight per day (50 per cent more than the RDA for younger adults). It's a good idea to have some protein at every meal and to spread your intake across the day. Aim for 25–30g (1oz) per meal.

GETTING PROTEIN FROM YOUR DIET

We can obtain the protein we need from plant as well as animal sources, so there's no need for vegetarians to worry about whether they are getting enough. For example, you might be surprised that even low-fat foods like Greek yoghurt (twice as much protein as regular yoghurt) and cottage cheese are excellent sources of protein, as are oats, peanut butter and lentils. And vegans who eat plenty of legumes (beans and

lentils) and a varied plant-based diet can maintain their muscle mass and stay fit and healthy.

Animal products are complete proteins, which means they contain all of the nine essential amino acids that we can only obtain from food. They include meat, poultry, fish, shellfish, eggs, cheese, yoghurt and dairy products.

Plant proteins – with the exception of soya beans and quinoa – are incomplete, so you need to eat as varied a diet as possible to get the whole range of amino acids. If you're vegan, there's no need to worry as you can enjoy lentils, chickpeas, beans, nuts and nut butters, quinoa, whole grains, seeds, tofu, tempeh, seitan, spirulina, potatoes and dark green leafy vegetables. Many other vegetables (including broccoli, spinach and avocado) and fruit (apricots and blackberries) also contain small amounts of protein.

NOTE: Lean protein contains fewer calories than carbs and fat and it helps you to lose weight and/or maintain a healthy weight by making you feel full and curbing your appetite, so you're less likely to snack on carbs in between meals.

ARE YOU GETTING ENOUGH PROTEIN?

Some of the warning signs that you might not be getting enough include:

– Hair, nail and skin problems.
– Fatigue and feeling weak.
– Loss of muscle mass.
– Feeling hungry.
– Injuries that are slow to heal.
– Swelling in the abdomen, legs, feet and hands.
– Mood changes.
– Increased susceptibility to colds and viruses.

If you have any of these symptoms, talk to your doctor or nutritionist.

PROTEIN POWDER

People use protein powders as a nutritional supplement for a variety of reasons: for muscle growth and performance; speeding up recovery after exercise and repairing damaged tissue; or for nutritional purposes if they have a requirement for additional protein. This group includes older people and those who have a chronic illness or are recovering from one. However, you can get all the protein your body needs without using supplements if you eat a healthy varied diet.

There are several types of protein powder, including the following:

WHEY: This is the most popular and is made from the proteins in liquid milk left over from cheese making. It is a complete protein, containing all nine essential amino acids, and is absorbed quickly.

CASEIN: Another dairy protein, it contains glutamine for speedy muscle recovery after working out.

HEMP: Derived from hemp seeds, this is favoured by people who are allergic to dairy as well as vegans. However, it is not a complete protein.

SOY: This is a complete protein, plus it's dairy-free and suitable for vegans.

If buying protein powder check the ingredients on the label. Many contain additives such as sugars and thickeners, and a few have traces of heavy metals and pesticides. Flavourings make them more palatable, especially when you're adding them to smoothies and shakes, but opt for low-sugar, low-calorie brands.

You can add protein powder to drinks, porridge, chia pudding, breakfast pancakes, dips, home-baked bread, cookies, cakes and muffins, protein energy balls and bars, smoothies and milkshakes. See the recipes in the protein powder section of this book.

SNACKS

Changing your go-to snacks can help to boost your protein intake. When you feel hungry between meals, just grab a high-protein snack. It will release appetite-suppressing hormones, slow your digestion and stabilise your blood sugar levels.

PROTEINS AT A GLANCE

VEGETABLE PROTEINS

VEGETABLES: Peas, green beans, Brussels sprouts, broccoli, spinach, asparagus, corn, sweet potatoes, potatoes, artichokes, Chinese cabbage, cauliflower.

BEANS AND PULSES: Edamame, soya, haricot, green, runner, borlotti, cannellini, black, kidney, mung, pinto, broad (fava) and butter (lima) beans, chickpeas, split peas, lentils, alfalfa sprouts.

NUTS: Almonds, Brazil nuts, cashews, chestnuts, coconut, hazelnuts, macadamia nuts, peanuts, pecans, pine nuts, pistachios, walnuts, nut milks and yoghurts, nut butters.

SEEDS: Chia, hemp, linseed, pumpkin, sesame, sunflower, seed butters, tahini.

SOYA-BASED FOODS: Tofu, seitan, tempeh, soy milk and yoghurt.

GRAINS: Quinoa, wild rice, spelt, buckwheat, amaranth, millet, kamut, teff, oats, oatmeal, cornmeal, wholegrain pasta, couscous, brown rice, barley, wheat.

FRUIT: Avocados, raspberries, blackberries, apricots (fresh and dried), jackfruit, prunes, raisins, guavas, kiwi fruit, oranges, bananas, peaches, cantaloupe melon.

PLUS: Nutritional yeast, spirulina, protein powder.

ANIMAL PROTEINS

MEAT: Beef, lamb, pork, ham, game – e.g. venison, rabbit.

POULTRY: Chicken, duck, turkey, game – e.g. pheasant.

OFFAL: Liver, kidneys.

WHITE FISH: Cod, haddock, halibut, sole, mullet, sea bass, sea bream.

OILY FISH: Salmon, tuna, mackerel, herring, sardines.

SHELLFISH: Crab, lobster, prawns (shrimp), scallops, mussels, clams, squid.

DAIRY PRODUCTS: Eggs, cheese, cottage cheese, milk, yoghurt (especially Greek yoghurt), kefir, butter, cream.

PROTEIN TIPS & GUIDELINES

– Choose lean protein sources that are low in saturated fats.
– Choose lean meat, such as chicken and turkey.
– Choose protein-rich snacks rather than carbs.
– Choose protein-rich vegetables.
– Choose wholegrain bread and cereals.
– Eat a variety of white and oily fish – fresh, frozen or canned.
– Eat some nuts and seeds every day.
– Eat a high-protein food at every meal.
– Eat protein before carbs to prevent high blood sugar levels.
– Eat a variety of protein-rich foods.
– Add protein to salads, soups and sandwiches.
– Replace sugary breakfast cereals with oats or eggs.
– Instead of sugary spreads, use nut and seed butters on toast.
– Avoid processed meats.

SNACKS
(5-20G PROTEIN)

SPICED CRISPY CHICKPEA SNACKS

SERVES: 6 | PREP: 10 MINUTES | COOK: 30-40 MINUTES

2 x 400g/14oz cans
    chickpeas, drained
    and rinsed
2 tbsp olive oil
½ tsp garlic salt or fine sea
    salt
1 tsp ground cumin
½ tsp ground coriander
½ tsp ground cinnamon
½ tsp sweet paprika
a good pinch of cayenne
    pepper

Crunchy, high-fibre roasted chickpeas are so easy to make if you use canned ones rather than cooking dried from scratch. You can grab a handful for a delicious pick-me-up between meals, serve them with drinks, or sprinkle them over salads and bowl food.

1 Preheat the oven to 190°C, 375°F, gas mark 5.

2 Dry the rinsed chickpeas by blotting them with kitchen paper (paper towels). Put them in a bowl with the olive oil and stir gently until they are coated and glistening with the oil.

3 Add the salt and spices and mix until the chickpeas are evenly coated.

4 Spread the chickpeas in a single layer in a large roasting tin (baking pan) and bake in the oven for 30–40 minutes, turning them halfway through, until crunchy and golden brown. Watch them carefully towards the end to prevent them burning.

5 Leave to cool in the tin before using. Once cold, they will stay fresh and crisp stored in a sealed container or plastic bag at room temperature for up to 5 days.

OR YOU CAN TRY THIS...
– For a real kick, add some hot chilli powder to the spice mix.
– For an Indian take, stir in a little ground turmeric and garam masala.
– You can use any vegetable oil, e.g. rapeseed (canola) or avocado oil.

TURKEY MAYO OPEN SANDWICH

SERVES: 4 | PREP: 5-10 MINUTES

13g
/SERVE

4 tbsp light mayonnaise
2 tsp mango chutney
1 small red bird's eye chilli,
   deseeded and diced
a few sprigs of coriander
   (cilantro), finely chopped
100g/3½oz cooked turkey
   breast, diced
1 small mango, peeled,
   stoned (pitted) and diced
4 slices high-protein bread
4 tsp seeds, e.g. pumpkin,
   cumin or fennel
salt and freshly ground
   black pepper

You can now buy high-protein bread loaves in most supermarkets. Most are made with wholemeal flour and mixed seeds, including linseed (flaxseed), pumpkin, sunflower and poppy seeds. A single 35g slice usually averages out at around 4.5g protein. Open sandwiches are easy to make for a quick snack.

1 In a small bowl, mix the mayonnaise with the chutney. Stir in the chilli, coriander, turkey and mango, then season to taste with salt and pepper.

2 Toast the bread, if wished, and spread the turkey mayo mixture over the top, right up to the edges.

3 Sprinkle with the seeds and serve immediately.

OR YOU CAN TRY THIS...
– Substitute diced chicken for the turkey.
– Use the turkey mayo mixture as a filling for sandwiches, wraps or pitta bread.
– Use papaya (pawpaw) or peaches instead of mango.
– Scatter with pine nuts instead of seeds.
– Add some raisins to the turkey mayo mixture.
– Substitute thick Greek yoghurt for the mayonnaise.

CHEESY REFRIED BEAN QUESADILLAS

16g /SERVE

SERVES: 4 | PREP: 15 MINUTES | COOK: 12-16 MINUTES

100g/3½oz (1 cup) grated
 Cheddar cheese
6 spring onions (scallions),
 thinly sliced
1 fresh or bottled jalapeño
 chilli, diced
1 small bunch of coriander
 (cilantro), chopped
1 x 400g/14oz can refried
 beans
1 ripe avocado, peeled,
 stoned (pitted) and diced
juice of 1 lime
4 large flour tortillas
spray olive oil
salt and freshly ground
 black pepper
chilli sauce, for drizzling

TIP: To make 4
individual quesadillas,
divide the filling
between the 4 tortillas,
spreading it over one
half, then fold the
tortilla over to encase
the filling and make
a half-moon shape.
Press down on the
edges to seal and cook
as per Step 4.

These spicy quesadillas make a great high-protein snack and are really
quick and easy to prepare and cook. If you don't have a can of refried
beans handy in your store cupboard, just rinse and drain some canned
kidney beans and smash them roughly before mixing with the other
filling ingredients.

1 In a bowl, mix together the grated cheese, spring onions, chilli
 and coriander. Stir in the refried beans and season lightly with salt
 and pepper.

2 In a separate bowl, sprinkle the avocado with the lime juice and
 stir gently to coat.

3 Spread the refried bean mixture evenly over 2 tortillas, leaving a
 thin border around the edges. Sprinkle with the avocado and place
 the other tortilla on top. Press firmly together around the edge.

4 Lightly spray a large non-stick frying pan (skillet) with oil and set over
 a medium heat. When it's really hot, carefully place a quesadilla in
 the pan and cook for 3 minutes or until crisp and golden underneath.
 Flip it over carefully and cook the other side. The filling should be
 hot and the cheese melting. Slide the quesadilla out of the pan and
 keep warm while you cook the rest in the same way.

5 Cut each quesadilla into 6 wedges. Eat immediately, drizzled with
 chilli sauce.

OR YOU CAN TRY THIS...
– Serve with some sour cream, yoghurt, guacamole or fresh salsa.
– Add some canned sweetcorn kernels to the filling.
– Instead of Cheddar, try grated Monterey Jack, Gruyère or mozzarella.

CHEESY MUSHROOM AND SPINACH PORRIDGE

10g
/SERVE

SERVES: 4 | PREP: 10 MINUTES | COOK: 25-30 MINUTES

3 tbsp olive oil
15g/½oz (1 tbsp) unsalted
    butter
1 onion, finely chopped
450g/1lb white or chestnut
    mushrooms, thinly sliced
150g/5oz (generous 1½ cups)
    oatmeal
900ml/1½ pints (3¾ cups)
    vegetable stock
200g/7oz baby spinach
    leaves
115g/4oz (1 cup) grated
    Cheddar cheese
salt and freshly ground
    black pepper

Oats are not only a good source of protein but are also low GI, helping to regulate your blood sugar levels and release energy more slowly throughout the day. It makes the perfect food for athletes, especially endurance runners. You can enjoy this delicious savoury porridge as a nutritious snack or even for breakfast or brunch.

1 Heat the olive oil and butter in a non-stick pan set over a low heat. Add the onion and cook, stirring occasionally, for 6–8 minutes until softened. Stir in the mushrooms and cook gently for 3 minutes or until tender and golden brown.

2 Add the oatmeal and stir for 1–2 minutes, then add the stock. Increase the heat to a gentle simmer and cook, stirring occasionally, for 10–15 minutes or until the oatmeal has absorbed all the liquid. The porridge should have the consistency of a moist risotto.

3 Stir in the spinach and when the leaves turn bright green and wilt into the porridge, add most of the Cheddar and season to taste with salt and pepper.

4 Divide between 4 shallow serving bowls and sprinkle with the remaining cheese. Serve immediately.

OR YOU CAN TRY THIS...
– For a real protein boost, top the porridge with a poached or fried egg. This will add approximately 6g protein per serving.
– Use shredded kale or spring greens instead of spinach.
– Use dried porcini mushrooms and add the soaking liquid to the stock.
– Add a handful of chopped herbs for a more aromatic and green-flecked porridge.

HIGH-PROTEIN SCRAMBLED EGG WRAPS

SERVES: 4 | PREP: 10 MINUTES | COOK: 8-10 MINUTES

17g /SERVE

1 tbsp olive oil
4 ripe tomatoes, chopped
6 medium free-range eggs
3 tbsp chia seeds
a handful of flat-leaf parsley
    or chives, chopped
4 wholewheat tortilla wraps
a handful of rocket (arugula)
1 ripe avocado, peeled,
    stoned (pitted) and diced
juice of ½ lime
salt and freshly ground
    black pepper

Chia seeds can be added to scrambled eggs to boost the protein content of these delicious wraps. Always use wholemeal or multiseed tortillas in preference to white as they have a higher protein content and are a better source of dietary fibre. You can eat these wraps as an on-the-go snack, or they're perfect for a leisurely weekend breakfast or brunch.

1 Heat the oil in a non-stick frying pan (skillet) and cook the tomatoes over a medium heat for 3–4 minutes until starting to soften.

2 Meanwhile, beat the eggs in a bowl with the chia seeds and herbs. Season lightly with salt and pepper.

3 Pour the egg mixture into the hot pan, reduce the heat and stir with a wooden spoon until the eggs start to scramble and set. Remove from the heat.

4 Meanwhile, heat the tortilla wraps in a low oven or one by one in a griddle (grill) pan.

5 Toss the rocket and avocado in the lime juice and scatter over the warm tortillas. Spoon the scrambled egg mixture on top and roll up or fold over to make parcels. Serve immediately.

OR YOU CAN TRY THIS...
– For Mexican-style wraps, add some crushed chilli flakes and serve with fresh salsa and sour cream.
– Omit the avocado and add a spoonful of guacamole instead.
– Add some grilled (broiled) sliced (bell) peppers, courgettes (zucchini) or mushrooms.

EGG AND BACON CUPS

MAKES: 8 | SERVES: 4 | PREP: 10 MINUTES | COOK: 15 MINUTES

16g /SERVE

olive oil, for brushing
8 thin rashers (slices) lean
    streaky or back bacon
8 medium free-range eggs
2 small tomatoes, deseeded
    and diced
a small bunch of chives,
    snipped
salt and freshly ground
    black pepper

The beauty of these little 'cups' is that they are high in protein and relatively low in fat and carbs. They're a great choice for an easy nutritious snack or breakfast when you're in a hurry. We recommend using thin bacon rashers as they crisp better than thicker ones.

1 Preheat the oven to 190°C/375°F/gas mark 5. Lightly brush a muffin tin (pan) with oil.

2 Line the sides of each muffin hole with a bacon rasher, wrapping it right round.

3 Break an egg into each muffin hole and sprinkle the diced tomato and chives over the top. Season with salt and pepper.

4 Bake in the oven for 15 minutes or until the bacon is cooked and crispy and the eggs are set.

5 Carefully run a knife around each muffin hole and turn out the bacon and egg cups. Eat immediately while they are piping hot.

OR YOU CAN TRY THIS...
– Use pancetta slices instead of bacon.
– Vary the herbs – try chopped parsley or dill.
– Sprinkle the top of each cup with 1 teaspoon grated Parmesan cheese – this will add 1.2g protein per serving (2 cups).

SNACK MINI 'QUICHES'

MAKES: 8 | SERVES: 4 | PREP: 15 MINUTES | COOK: 25-30 MINUTES

13g /SERVE

2 tbsp olive oil, plus extra
   for brushing
1 red onion, finely chopped
2 red or yellow (bell)
   peppers, deseeded and
   chopped
4 tomatoes, diced
200g baby spinach leaves
4 medium free-range eggs
120ml/4fl oz (½ cup) milk
200g/7oz low-fat cottage
   cheese
a handful of dill, finely
   chopped
salt and freshly ground
   black pepper

You can use low-fat or fat-free cottage cheese to make these nutritious 'no-pastry' snacks – it's a good source of protein but much lower in fat than regular cheese. Make these quiches in advance and store them in a sealed container in the fridge for 2–3 days. Eat for breakfast, take them to work or college as a packed lunch, or treat yourself when you're feeling peckish.

1 Preheat the oven to 190°C/375°F/gas mark 5.

2 Heat the oil in a frying pan (skillet) over a medium heat. Add the onion and peppers and cook for 6–8 minutes until softened. Stir in the tomatoes and spinach and cook for 2 minutes until the spinach wilts and turns bright green.

3 Lightly brush two 4-hole non-stick muffin tins (pans) with oil and divide the vegetable mixture between them.

4 In a bowl, whisk together the eggs and milk. Stir in the cottage cheese and dill and season with salt and pepper.

5 Pour the egg mixture over the vegetables and bake in the oven for 15–20 minutes until risen, golden brown and firm to the touch.

OR YOU CAN TRY THIS...
– Use chopped parsley, chives or coriander (cilantro) instead of dill.
– Add some chopped bacon or ham.
– Use diced mushrooms or squash instead of peppers.

CHICKEN SATAY SNACKS

20g
/SERVE

SERVES: 8 | PREP: 15 MINUTES | MARINATE: 30 MINUTES | COOK: 15 MINUTES

75ml/3fl oz (generous
    ¼ cup) coconut milk
1 tsp ground cumin
1 tsp ground turmeric
1 tsp ground coriander
2 garlic cloves, crushed
2 tsp brown sugar
a pinch of sea salt
500g/18oz skinned chicken
    breast fillets, cut into
    long strips

FOR THE SATAY DIP:
150g/5oz (generous ½ cup)
    crunchy peanut butter
1 garlic clove, crushed
1 tsp Thai red curry paste
1 tsp nam pla (Thai fish
    sauce)
150ml/¼ pint (generous ½
    cup) canned coconut milk
1 tbsp brown sugar or honey
juice of 1 lime

You can cook the chicken in advance and chill overnight to eat the
following day. It tastes equally good hot or cold. If you're serving this
on a warm summer day, you can cook the chicken over hot coals on
a barbecue for a really smoky, spicy flavour. Transform this dish into
supper for 4 people by serving it with boiled rice and a crisp salad and
you'll have a whopping 40g protein per serving.

1 In a large bowl, mix together the coconut milk, ground spices, garlic,
  sugar and salt. Stir in the chicken strips, then cover and leave in the
  fridge to marinate for at least 30 minutes.

2 Thread the chicken strips onto 8 pre-soaked thin wooden skewers
  (see below), weaving them through the chicken to make 'S' shapes.

3 Make the satay dip: put all the ingredients into a blender and blitz
  until well combined.

4 Cook the chicken skewers on a hot ridged griddle (grill) pan over a
  medium heat for about 15 minutes, turning occasionally, until golden
  brown, slightly charred and cooked right through. Serve hot or cold
  with the satay dip.

OR YOU CAN TRY THIS...
– Use palm sugar instead of brown sugar.
– Substitute turkey breast for the chicken.
– Add some grated fresh root ginger to the satay dip.
– Use sweet chilli sauce instead of curry paste.

TIP: Soak the wooden
skewers in cold water
for 10–15 minutes
before using to
prevent them burning
during cooking.

PROTEIN TRAIL MIX

SERVES: 6 | PREP: 10 MINUTES

11g
/SERVE

60g/2oz (scant ½ cup)
cashews
60g/2oz (scant ½ cup)
shelled pistachios
40g/1½oz (½ cup) coconut
flakes
40g/1½oz (scant ½ cup)
mixed sunflower and
pumpkin seeds
40g/1½oz (scant ½ cup)
sultanas (golden raisins)
40g/1½oz (¼ cup) dried
berries, e.g. cranberries,
blueberries, cherries
100g/3½oz (1 cup) high-
protein low-fat granola,
e.g. Protein nut butter
granola (see page 30)
100g/3½oz dark chocolate
(minimum 70% cocoa
solids), cut into small
chunks

Eat this as a high-energy snack, sprinkle over your breakfast cereal or use as a crunchy topping for yoghurt and smoothie bowls. Use raw nuts rather than shop-bought salted, roasted or candied ones. If you're going out trekking in a hot climate, you may wish to leave out the chocolate, which could soften or even melt.

1 Put all the ingredients in a bowl and mix well together.

2 Transfer to a Mason or Kilner jar or a Ziploc bag and seal. The trail mix will keep well stored in a cool, dry place for up to 3 weeks.

OR YOU CAN TRY THIS...

– Add some dried goji berries, chopped dates, apricots or figs.
– Use chocolate chips instead of chunks.
– Stir in some salty popcorn or a good pinch of sea salt for a sweet and salty mix.
– Add cacao nibs and omit the chocolate.
– Use peanuts instead of pistachios.

TIP: For a more distinctive flavour, you can toast the seeds and cashews. Just heat a dry frying pan (skillet) over a medium to high heat and add the nuts or seeds to the hot pan in a single layer. Cook for a few minutes, stirring or shaking occasionally, until they release their fragrance and are golden brown. Remove from the pan immediately before they catch and burn.

PROTEIN NUT BUTTER GRANOLA

SERVES: 6 | PREP: 10 MINUTES | COOK: 20-25 MINUTES

11g
/SERVE

30g/1oz (2 tbsp) coconut oil
60g/2oz (¼ cup) peanut
   butter
2 tbsp maple syrup
1 tsp vanilla extract
200g/7oz (2½ cups) rolled
   oats
50g/2oz (½ cup) chopped
   nuts, e.g. hazelnuts,
   pecans
25g/1oz (scant ¼ cup)
   sunflower seeds
25g/1oz (scant ¼ cup)
   pumpkin seeds
2 tbsp chia seeds
50g/2oz (scant ½ cup)
   raisins
a good pinch of sea salt

This makes 6 servings but you can easily double the quantities and make
a larger batch. It will keep well in an airtight container for a couple of
weeks. There are no hard-and-fast rules about what you put in, so be
adventurous and use whatever you've got to hand. Serve it as a snack or
use it as a sprinkle, or stir into dairy-free soya or coconut yoghurt and
top with fresh berries or sliced banana. For a higher protein content, you
can add 30g/1oz protein powder to the mix before baking, which will
add 3.5g protein per serving.

1 Preheat the oven to 170°C/325°F/gas mark 3. Line a large baking tray
   (cookie sheet) with baking parchment.

2 Heat the coconut oil, peanut butter, maple syrup and vanilla extract
   in a pan set over a low heat. When the coconut oil melts, stir in the
   oats, nuts, seeds, raisins and salt. Make sure that everything is well
   coated and break up with your hands into small clumps.

3 Spread out in a thin layer on the lined baking tray and bake in the
   oven for 20–25 minutes, stirring once or twice, until golden brown
   and crisp. Leave to cool before transferring to an airtight container
   and storing in a cool, dry place.

OR YOU CAN TRY THIS...
– Serve with regular milk, soya or nut milk and seasonal fruits.
– Add some shredded coconut, cacao nibs, dried cranberries or
   chopped dates.
– Vary the nuts: try chopped almonds, pistachios or walnuts.
– Use almond or cashew nut butter instead of peanut.

CHICKEN AND HUMMUS LETTUCE WRAPS

SERVES: 4 | PREP: 10 MINUTES

12g
/SERVE

200g/7oz cooked chicken
   breast fillets, diced
115g/4oz (½ cup) hummus
1 garlic clove, crushed
juice of ½ lemon
a handful of coriander
   (cilantro), finely chopped
4 large crisp iceberg lettuce
   leaves
2 large carrots, coarsely
   grated
salt and freshly ground
   black pepper
sweet chilli sauce,
   for drizzling

The beauty of this high-protein snack is that you can make it in minutes. Crisp iceberg lettuce leaves are best for wraps and parcels as they are large enough to enclose the filling and do not tear easily, unlike other lettuces.

1 Put the chicken, hummus, garlic and lemon juice in a bowl and mix well. Stir in the coriander.

2 Divide the mixture between the lettuce leaves and top with the grated carrots. Season lightly with salt and pepper.

3 Fold the sides of the lettuce leaves over the filling in the centre, and then fold the ends over too to make 4 neat parcels. Turn them over and place seam-side down.

4 Serve immediately, drizzled with sweet chilli sauce.

OR YOU CAN TRY THIS...
– Stir some Greek yoghurt into the chicken mixture to make it creamier.
– Add some diced avocado and use lime juice instead of lemon.
– Instead of grated carrot, use roasted sliced (bell) peppers.
– Substitute diced feta cheese for the chicken and you will have 9.5g protein per wrap.

REALLY GREEN FALAFELS

SERVES: 4 | PREP: 15 MINUTES | COOK: 4–5 MINUTES

15g
/SERVE

200g/7oz canned chickpeas, rinsed and drained
200g/7oz (1¼ cups) frozen peas, defrosted
45g/1½oz baby spinach leaves
4 spring onions (scallions), finely chopped
a bunch of flat-leaf parsley, stalks removed
a bunch of coriander (cilantro), stalks removed
5 garlic cloves, peeled
1 green chilli, deseeded
1 tsp ground cumin
1 tsp ground coriander
4 tbsp gram (chickpea) flour
½ tsp baking powder
vegetable oil, for frying
sea salt flakes

FOR THE TAHINI SAUCE:
100g/3½oz (½ cup) tahini paste
3 garlic cloves, peeled
a pinch of ground cumin
½ tsp sea salt
juice of 1 lemon
1 tbsp olive oil
cold water, to mix

Most falafels are a neutral and unappetisingly brown colour, so these intensely green ones are a revelation. The frozen peas add protein as well as flavour and colour. You can eat these falafels as a healthy snack or use as a filling for wraps, pitta pockets and panini.

1 Blitz the chickpeas, peas, spinach, spring onions, herbs, garlic, chilli and ground spices in a blender until you have a thick paste. Transfer to a bowl and stir in the flour and baking powder until evenly combined.

2 Divide the mixture into small pieces (about 20) and mould each one into a ball.

3 Make the tahini sauce: blitz the tahini, garlic, cumin, salt and lemon juice in a blender until smooth. Add some cold water, a little at a time, until you have the desired consistency – neither too thick nor too thin.

4 Pour the vegetable oil into a saucepan to a depth of 5cm (2in) and set over a high heat. When it reaches 170°C/325°F, reduce the heat and start frying the falafels, a few at a time, for 4–5 minutes until crisp and golden brown all over. Remove from the pan with a slotted spoon and drain on kitchen paper (paper towels). Sprinkle them with sea salt.

5 Serve the hot falafels with the tahini sauce.

OR YOU CAN TRY THIS...
– Use shredded kale or spring greens instead of spinach.
– Stir a little Greek yoghurt into the tahini sauce to make it creamier.

TIP: If you don't have a sugar thermometer to test the temperature of the oil, just drop a small piece of the falafel mixture into the pan of hot oil – if it sizzles and turns brown, it's ready.

LIGHT MEALS & SALADS
(15–35G PROTEIN)

SALMON, QUINOA AND PESTO SALAD

34g
/SERVE

SERVES: 4 | PREP: 15 MINUTES | COOK: 15 MINUTES

400g/14oz skinned
　　salmon fillets
200g/7oz (1¼ cups) quinoa
　　(raw weight)
2 tbsp olive oil, plus extra
　　for brushing
grated zest and juice of
　　1 lemon
115g/4oz (1½ cups) frozen
　　soya beans, defrosted
1 small bunch of spring
　　onions (scallions),
　　chopped
a handful of flat-leaf parsley,
　　finely chopped
1 tbsp chia seeds
1 tbsp black sesame seeds
4 tbsp fresh pesto
salt and freshly ground
　　black pepper

It's not only the salmon that provides protein in this delicious salad; quinoa is a great source of vegetable protein and dietary fibre, as are soya beans.

1 Preheat the oven to 180°C, 350°F, gas mark 4.

2 Put the salmon fillets on a large piece of kitchen foil and fold it over loosely to make a parcel, sealing the edges. Place on a baking tray (cookie sheet) and cook in the oven for about 15 minutes until the salmon is tender and cooked through. Remove from the foil and break up into large flakes.

3 Meanwhile, cook the quinoa according to the instructions on the packet.

4 Stir the 2 tablespoons of olive oil, the lemon zest and juice into the hot quinoa. Mix in the soya beans, spring onions, most of the parsley and the seeds. Season to taste and divide between 4 shallow serving bowls.

5 Add the salmon and sprinkle with the remaining parsley. Drizzle with the pesto and serve warm.

OR YOU CAN TRY THIS...
– Instead of soya beans, use canned flageolet, borlotti or kidney beans.
– Top with some sliced avocado and a drizzle of chilli sauce instead of pesto.
– Experiment with different herbs: coriander (cilantro), chives or dill.

BBQ CHICKEN SALAD

SERVES: 4 | PREP: 15 MINUTES | COOK: 25-30 MINUTES

30g
/SERVE

1 tsp coriander seeds
2 tsp cumin seeds
2 large sweet potatoes, peeled and cut into chunks
2 red onions, cut into wedges
2 large red or yellow (bell) peppers, deseeded and sliced
3 tbsp olive oil
4 x 115g/4oz chicken breast fillets (skin on)
150g/5oz washed mixed salad leaves
30g/1oz (¼ cup) toasted pine nuts
balsamic vinegar, for drizzling
salt and freshly ground black pepper

FOR THE LEMONY POPPY SEED DRESSING:
3 tbsp olive oil
1 tbsp white wine vinegar
juice of 1 lemon
1 garlic clove, crushed
1 tsp grated fresh root ginger
1 tsp honey mustard
1 tsp poppy seeds

Chicken always tastes best when it's cooked over hot coals on the barbecue until it's crisp, charred and smoky on the outside, and juicy and succulent on the inside. It's one of the best sources of protein and very lean – most of the fat is in the skin. If you're watching your weight and trying to reduce the fats you consume, you can remove the skin before cooking, but the chicken won't be as moist.

1 Preheat the oven to 200°C, 400°F, gas mark 6.

2 Coarsely grind the coriander and cumin seeds using a pestle and mortar or seed grinder. Put the sweet potatoes, red onions and peppers in a roasting tin (pan) and drizzle with the olive oil. Sprinkle the ground seeds over the top and season with salt and pepper.

3 Roast in the oven for 25–30 minutes, turning once or twice, until the vegetables are tender and golden brown.

4 Meanwhile, cook the chicken over hot coals on the barbecue, turning it once or twice, for about 15 minutes until golden brown and cooked right through. When you insert a skewer the juices should run clear. Remove and cut into thick slices.

5 Blitz all the dressing ingredients in a blender until smooth. Alternatively, whisk them together in a small bowl.

6 Put the roasted vegetables and salad leaves in a bowl and toss lightly with the dressing. Divide between 4 serving plates and sprinkle with the pine nuts. Lay the chicken on top and drizzle with balsamic vinegar.

OR YOU CAN TRY THIS...

– Instead of sweet potato use pumpkin, butternut squash, beetroot (beets) or carrots.
– Vary the seeds: try fennel or hemp seeds.
– Use any salad leaves: lettuce, watercress, baby spinach, rocket (arugula) or radicchio.

WINTER CHICORY AND BLUE CHEESE SALAD

17g
/SERVE

SERVES: 4 | PREP: 15 MINUTES | COOK: 2-3 MINUTES

100g/3½oz fine green
   beans, trimmed
2 large heads white chicory
   (Belgian endive)
1 radicchio, leaves torn
   into large pieces
2 red apples
1 bunch of spring onions
   (scallions), finely
   chopped
1 ripe large avocado, peeled,
   stoned (pitted) and
   cubed
1 x 400g/14oz can (2 cups)
   cannellini beans, rinsed
   and drained
115g/4oz blue cheese, e.g.
   Roquefort or Stilton,
   diced or crumbled
60g/2oz (½ cup) chopped
   walnuts
1 small bunch of flat-leaf
   parsley, finely chopped

**FOR THE HONEY MUSTARD
   DRESSING:**
4 tbsp olive oil
1 tbsp cider vinegar
2 tsp honey mustard
juice of 1 lemon
salt and freshly ground
   black pepper

This colourful salad is an excellent way to boost your vegetable protein.
The beans, nuts, cheese and even the avocado will all make a valuable
contribution to your daily intake.

1 Cook the green beans in a pan of boiling water for 2–3 minutes until
   just tender but still slightly crisp with some 'bite'. Drain and refresh
   in cold water. Drain well, pat dry with kitchen paper (paper towels)
   and set aside.

2 Trim the fat bases off the chicory and radicchio and thinly slice the
   heads into rounds. Core the apples and cut them into small cubes.

3 Mix the chicory, radicchio, apples, green beans, spring onions,
   avocado, cannellini beans, cheese, walnuts and parsley in a bowl.

4 Make the dressing: blend the olive oil and vinegar with the honey
   mustard and lemon juice and season to taste with salt and pepper.

5 Lightly toss the chicory salad in the dressing and serve immediately.

OR YOU CAN TRY THIS...
– Use cubed or sliced juicy pears instead of apples.
– Opt for a creamy blue cheese: Gorgonzola, dolcelatte or Cambozola.
– Any canned beans will work well: try butter beans (lima beans),
   chickpeas or kidney beans.

BAKED STUFFED AUBERGINES AND PEPPERS

SERVES: 4 | PREP: 15 MINUTES | COOK: 20 MINUTES

16g /SERVE

2 large aubergines
   (eggplants)
2 large red, green or yellow
   (bell) peppers
4 tbsp olive oil
225g/8oz (1½ cups)
   buckwheat (kasha)
   (raw weight)
1 large onion, finely
   chopped
2 garlic cloves, crushed
3 ripe tomatoes, diced
a handful of flat-leaf parsley,
   chopped
60g/2oz (½ cup) pine nuts
30g/1oz mixed seeds, e.g.
   sunflower, chia, fennel,
   caraway, cumin
grated zest and juice of
   1 lemon
100g/3½oz (1 cup) grated
   Cheddar cheese
salt and freshly ground
   black pepper

These baked stuffed vegetables are delicious served hot, lukewarm or even cold. The buckwheat, pine nuts and seeds add crunch as well as protein. You don't have to top them with Cheddar – any grated cheese works well or even some crumbled feta or goat's cheese.

1 Preheat the oven to 200°C, 400°F, gas mark 6.

2 Cut the aubergines and peppers in half lengthways through the stalks. Scoop out the inside of the aubergines and dice the flesh. Discard the seeds inside the peppers. Put the scooped-out aubergine and pepper shells, cut-side up, in a roasting tin (pan) and sprinkle with 2 tablespoons of the olive oil. Bake in the oven for 20 minutes or until tender. Remove and cool.

3 Meanwhile, prepare all the filling ingredients. Cook the buckwheat according to the instructions on the packet.

4 Heat the remaining olive oil in a frying pan (skillet) over a low heat and cook the onion and garlic, stirring occasionally, for 6–8 minutes until softened. Increase the heat to medium and add the diced aubergine, tomatoes and parsley. Cook for 5 minutes until tender. Season to taste with salt and pepper.

5 Toast the pine nuts in a small frying pan set over a medium heat for 1–2 minutes, tossing a few times, until fragrant and golden brown. Remove immediately.

6 Stir the cooked buckwheat, pine nuts, seeds, lemon zest and juice into the onion and tomato mixture. Use to fill the baked aubergine and pepper halves and sprinkle the Cheddar over the top.

7 Bake in the oven for 8–10 minutes until the cheese has melted and the topping is crisp and golden brown.

OR YOU CAN TRY THIS...
– Add a dash of harissa to the filling or serve with chilli sauce.

SHAWARMA CHICKEN AND AUBERGINE WRAPS

SERVES: 4 | PREP: 10 MINUTES | MARINATE: 30 MINUTES | COOK: 15-20 MINUTES

400g/14oz skinned chicken breast fillets
1 x 200g/7oz can (¾ cup) chickpeas, rinsed and drained
1 garlic clove, crushed
3 tbsp olive oil
a good squeeze of lemon juice
1 tsp cumin seeds, crushed
1 large aubergine (eggplant), cubed
4 large wholewheat wraps
100g/3½oz (scant ½ cup) Greek yoghurt
harissa or hot sauce, to serve

You can use any wraps to make this dish, but wholemeal or multiseed ones are the best choice as they contain more protein and fibre. Marinating the chicken before cooking tenderises it as well as adding flavour – you can even do it the day before and leave it in the fridge overnight.

1 Make the marinade: dry-fry the ground spices in a frying pan (skillet) for 1–2 minutes until they release their fragrance. Tip them into a large bowl and stir in the lemon juice, olive oil, garlic and coriander. Season with salt and pepper.

2 Add the chicken and coat with the marinade. Leave to stand at room temperature for 30 minutes.

3 Meanwhile, coarsely mash the chickpeas with the garlic, 1 tablespoon of the olive oil, the lemon juice and crushed cumin seeds. Season to taste.

4 Heat the remaining olive oil in a ridged griddle (grill) pan set over a medium to high heat. Add the aubergine and cook for 4–5 minutes, turning occasionally, until tender and golden brown all over. Remove and drain on kitchen paper (paper towels).

FOR THE SPICY MARINADE:

1 tsp sumac

½ tsp ras el hanout

½ tsp ground turmeric

½ tsp ground cumin

½ tsp sweet paprika

a pinch of ground cinnamon

juice of ½ lemon

2 tbsp olive oil

2 garlic cloves, crushed

a few sprigs of coriander
   (cilantro), chopped

salt and freshly ground
   black pepper

5 Add the chicken to the hot pan and cook for 10 minutes, turning occasionally, or until golden brown and cooked right through. Remove and cut into thin slices.

6 Heat the wraps in the griddle pan or a low oven. Spread the mashed chickpeas over them and top with the aubergine and chicken. Spoon over the yoghurt and roll up or fold over. Serve with harissa or hot sauce.

OR YOU CAN TRY THIS...

– Use diced lean lamb fillet instead of chicken.
– Spread the wraps with hummus rather than mashed chickpeas.
– Split some large wholewheat pitta breads and fill with the chicken, chickpeas and aubergine.
– Add some salad leaves to the wraps.

VIETNAMESE STEAK BAGUETTES

SERVES: 4 | PREP: 20 MINUTES | STAND: AT LEAST 1 HOUR | COOK: 10 MINUTES

33g
/SERVE

120g/4oz (½ cup) mayonnaise

2 spring onions (scallions), diced

2 tbsp hot sauce, e.g. Sriracha or sweet chilli

2 carrots, cut into thin matchsticks

4 radishes, thinly sliced

1 yellow or red (bell) pepper, deseeded and thinly sliced

1 small ridged cucumber, thinly sliced

4 tbsp rice vinegar

4 tbsp caster (superfine) sugar

1 tbsp nam pla (Thai fish sauce)

1 tbsp vegetable oil

4 x 100g/3½oz thin-cut steaks, all visible fat removed

4 small baguettes (French sticks)

The most delicious 'sandwich' of all time, this takes longer to make than most but is well worth the extra effort. We have used Sriracha but you can substitute your favourite hot sauce – sweet chilli sauce works really well.

1 Mix together the mayonnaise, spring onions and hot sauce in a bowl. Cover and chill in the fridge.

2 Put the carrots, radishes, pepper and cucumber in a heatproof bowl. Heat the vinegar and sugar in a small pan, stirring until the sugar dissolves, then bring to the boil and remove from the heat. Stir in the nam pla and pour over the vegetables in the bowl. Leave to stand for 1 hour.

3 Just before you're ready to eat, heat the oil in a frying pan (skillet) or griddle (grill) pan set over a medium to high heat. Add the steaks and cook for 2–3 minutes each side. Remove from the pan and cut into thin strips.

4 Split the baguettes in half lengthwise and scoop out some of the soft bread in the centre to leave a crusty shell. Spread the mayonnaise over the bases and add the steak slices. Top with the carrot and radish mixture, then cover with the baguette tops, pressing down firmly. Eat immediately while the steak is still warm.

OR YOU CAN TRY THIS...
– Add some pickled chillies, chopped coriander (cilantro) or crushed garlic to the filling.
– Stir some crushed chilli flakes or diced bird's eye chillies into the mayo as an alternative to hot sauce.

QUICK CHICKEN NOODLE LAKSA

SERVES: 4 | PREP: 10 MINUTES | COOK: 15-20 MINUTES

30g
/SERVE

1 tbsp groundnut (peanut)
  oil
1 bunch of spring onions
  (scallions), sliced
2 garlic cloves, crushed
2 tsp diced fresh root ginger
2 red chillies, thinly sliced
1 stalk lemongrass, peeled
  and diced
1 tbsp Thai green curry
  paste
1 tsp ground turmeric
1 litre/1¾ pints (4 cups)
  hot chicken stock
200ml/7fl oz (1 cup)
  canned coconut milk
400g/14oz cooked chicken
  breast fillets, shredded
1 tbsp nam pla (Thai fish
  sauce)
150g/5oz fine rice noodles
  (dry weight)
100g/3½oz (1 cup)
  beansprouts
juice of 1 lime
chopped coriander
  (cilantro), to garnish

This spicy soup will warm you up on a cold day, and the protein in the chicken helps provide a steady source of energy. For the best flavour and maximum nutritional benefits, use home-made chicken stock or a packet of ready-made stock rather than a bouillon cube.

1 Heat the oil in a large pan and stir-fry the spring onions, garlic, ginger, chillies and lemongrass over a medium to high heat for 2–3 minutes. Stir in the curry paste and turmeric and cook for 1 minute without burning.

2 Add the hot chicken stock and coconut milk and bring to the boil. Reduce the heat and simmer gently for 5 minutes. Add the chicken and nam pla and cook for 5 minutes.

3 Meanwhile, cook the rice noodles according to the instructions on the packet and drain well.

4 Stir them into the laksa with the beansprouts. Heat through gently for 2–3 minutes and then stir in the lime juice.

5 Divide between 4 shallow bowls and serve sprinkled with coriander.

OR YOU CAN TRY THIS...
– Use egg noodles instead of rice noodles.
– Add sliced mushrooms, carrot matchsticks, thin green beans, asparagus or some baby spinach leaves.
– Substitute Thai basil for the coriander.

TIP: Make up double the quantity and freeze the leftover soup before adding the noodles.

SPICY LAYERED PROTEIN POTS

SERVES: 4 | PREP: 20 MINUTES | COOK: 20-25 MINUTES

31g
/SERVE

300g/10oz cooked chicken,
    shredded
100g/3½ oz baby plum
    tomatoes, diced
¼ cucumber, diced
4 tbsp Greek yoghurt
1 tbsp spicy mango chutney
salt and freshly ground
    black pepper

FOR THE LENTIL LAYERS:
200g/7oz (1 cup) Puy or
    green lentils (dry weight)
1 tbsp vegetable oil
1 small red onion, diced
2 garlic cloves, crushed
2 tsp grated fresh root
    ginger
1 red chilli, diced
½ tsp ground turmeric
½ tsp ground cumin
4 tbsp chicken or vegetable
    stock
juice of 1 lime
a few sprigs of coriander
    (cilantro), chopped

You can take these little pots to work or college with you as a packed lunch, or eat them after a workout or exercise session. You will need four pots in which to assemble the layers – use individual glass jars or plastic containers.

1 Cook the lentils in a pan of simmering water for 20–25 minutes until just tender. They should hold their shape and not be mushy. Drain well in a sieve.

2 Meanwhile, heat the oil in a frying pan (skillet) set over a low to medium heat. Add the onion, garlic, ginger and chilli and cook for 6–8 minutes until softened. Stir in the ground spices and cook for 1 minute. Stir in the drained lentils and stock and simmer gently for 5 minutes. Add the lime juice and coriander. Season with salt and pepper and leave to cool.

3 When the lentils are cold, assemble the pots. Put half the lentils in the bottom of each pot and cover with the chicken, tomatoes and cucumber. Cover with the remaining lentils.

4 Mix the yoghurt and chutney together in a small bowl and use to top the pots. Serve immediately or cover and keep in the fridge for a few hours or overnight.

OR YOU CAN TRY THIS...
– Add some rocket (arugula), watercress or other salad leaves.
– Instead of chutney, stir some sweet chilli sauce or Sriracha into the yoghurt.

THAI TOFU AND PEANUT SALAD

SERVES: 4 | PREP: 20 MINUTES | COOK: 5 MINUTES

200g/7oz rice noodles
(dry weight)
2 carrots, cut into thin
matchsticks or strips
100g/3½oz mangetout
(snow peas), trimmed
and halved lengthways
1 bunch of spring onions
(scallions), sliced
½ cucumber, cut into
thin strips
a few crisp cos (romaine)
lettuce leaves
1 avocado, peeled, stoned
(pitted) and cubed
400g/14oz extra-firm tofu,
cut into 2.5cm (1in) cubes
1 tbsp light soy sauce
1 tbsp groundnut (peanut) oil
a handful of coriander
(cilantro), chopped
60g/2oz (scant ½ cup)
chopped roasted peanuts
sweet chilli sauce, for
drizzling

This vegan-friendly salad of fried tofu, noodles and crunchy vegetables is tossed in a creamy peanut butter dressing. The chilli in the dressing and the drizzle adds heat and intensity. Tofu is a useful source of protein for vegetarians and vegans and is delicious crisply fried.

1 Make the peanut butter dressing: blitz all the ingredients together in a blender until smooth and creamy. If it's too thick, add a little water.

2 Soak the rice noodles in plenty of cold water according to the instructions on the packet. Drain well.

3 Put the carrots, mangetout, spring onions, cucumber, lettuce and avocado in a bowl and mix gently together.

4 Put the tofu in a bowl with the soy sauce and stir gently. Heat the oil in a non-stick frying pan (skillet) set over a medium to high heat, and cook the tofu for 4–5 minutes, turning occasionally, until golden brown all over. Remove and drain on kitchen paper (paper towels).

5 Mix the vegetables, coriander and rice noodles together and toss gently in the peanut butter dressing. Divide between 4 shallow serving dishes. Arrange the tofu on top and sprinkle with the peanuts. Serve warm drizzled with sweet chilli sauce.

FOR THE PEANUT BUTTER DRESSING:

4 tbsp smooth peanut butter
1 tsp grated fresh root ginger
1 garlic clove, crushed
1 tbsp groundnut (peanut) oil
juice of 1 lime
1 tbsp light soy sauce or
    nam pla (Thai fish sauce)
2 tsp soft brown sugar
a pinch of crushed chilli flakes

OR YOU CAN TRY THIS...

– Use crunchy peanut butter instead of smooth in the dressing.
– Vary the vegetables: try shredded Chinese (Napa) cabbage, beansprouts, fine green beans or broccoli florets.

NOTE: If you're vegan, use soy sauce to make the dressing rather than nam pla.

JAPANESE SEARED TUNA SALAD

SERVES: 4 | PREP: 15 MINUTES | COOK: 15–20 MINUTES

34g
/SERVE

225g/8oz (1 cup) brown rice
(dry weight)
100g/3½oz (1¼ cups)
frozen edamame beans
150g/5oz (2¼ cups)
sprouted seeds, e.g.
mizuna, mung, radish
4 spring onions (scallions),
sliced diagonally
a large handful of baby
spinach leaves
1 avocado, peeled, stoned
(pitted) and diced
light olive oil, for brushing
4 x 100g/3½oz tuna steaks
1 sheet ready-toasted sushi
nori, cut into thin strips
2 tbsp toasted black sesame
seeds

FOR THE DRESSING:
2 tbsp vegetable oil,
e.g. rapeseed (canola)
1 tbsp toasted sesame oil
1 tbsp rice vinegar
2 tsp light soy sauce
1 tsp wasabi paste
juice of ½ lime
1 garlic clove, crushed
1 tsp grated fresh root ginger
2 tsp caster (superfine) sugar

This makes a satisfyingly filling light lunch or you could serve this with some cooked green vegetables for supper. The combination of tuna, brown rice and beans really boosts your protein intake.

1 Cook the brown rice according to the instructions on the packet.

2 Meanwhile, cook the beans in a pan of boiling water for 3 minutes until just tender. Refresh under running cold water, then drain.

3 Make the dressing: whisk all the ingredients together in a bowl until well blended, or shake vigorously in a screwtop jar.

4 Gently stir the rice with a fork to break up any clumps and separate the grains. Mix in the cooked beans, sprouted seeds, spring onions, spinach and avocado and toss gently in most of the dressing.

5 Lightly brush a non-stick griddle (grill) pan with oil and set over a medium to high heat. When it's really hot, add the tuna and cook for 2–3 minutes each side, depending on how well cooked you like it. Remove and cut into slices.

6 Divide the rice between 4 serving plates and top with the tuna. Drizzle the remaining dressing over the tuna and sprinkle with the nori and sesame seeds.

OR YOU CAN TRY THIS...
– Add some sliced radishes, cucumber, red or yellow (bell) peppers and chopped coriander (cilantro).
– Use salmon instead of tuna or even canned tuna, broken into chunks.

TIP: This is a delicious way of using up leftover cooked rice.

TUSCAN BEAN SOUP

SERVES: 4 | PREP: 15 MINUTES | COOK: 1 HOUR

32g
/SERVE

3 tbsp olive oil
1 large onion, finely chopped
1 leek, cleaned, trimmed
  and chopped
3 celery sticks, chopped
2 large carrots, diced
2 garlic cloves, crushed
1.2 litres/2 pints (5 cups)
  hot vegetable stock
450g/1lb ripe tomatoes,
  chopped
2 large potatoes, peeled and
  cubed
a few sprigs of thyme and
  rosemary
2 x 400g/14oz cans (3 cups)
  cannellini or borlotti
  beans, rinsed and drained
300g/10oz cavolo nero,
  ribs and stems removed,
  leaves shredded
4 tbsp fresh green pesto
salt and freshly ground
  black pepper

FOR THE PARMESAN CRISPS:
100g/3½oz (1 cup) grated
  Parmesan cheese

This earthy soup is so filling that it can also be eaten with crusty wholemeal or granary bread as a main meal. Or you can add some soup pasta for the last 10 minutes of cooking. The beans, potato, cavolo nero, pesto and Parmesan crisps are all excellent sources of vegetarian protein.

1 Heat the oil in a large pan set over a low heat and cook the onion, leek, celery, carrots and garlic, stirring occasionally, for 8–10 minutes until softened but not coloured.

2 Add the stock, tomatoes, potatoes and herbs and bring to the boil. Reduce the heat and simmer gently for 45 minutes, until all the vegetables are cooked and tender.

3 Add the beans and cavolo nero and cook for 5 minutes until the cabbage wilts but still has some bite and looks fresh. Season to taste with salt and pepper.

4 Meanwhile, make the Parmesan crisps. Preheat the oven to 180°C, 350°F, gas mark 4 and line a baking tray (cookie sheet) with baking parchment. Place 4 circular heaps of grated Parmesan on the paper, spaced well apart, and bake for 5 minutes or until the cheese melts and spreads. Remove from the oven before they start to brown, then set aside to cool and crisp up.

5 Divide the soup between 4 bowls and serve topped with a spoonful of pesto and the Parmesan crisps.

OR YOU CAN TRY THIS...
– Substitute 400g/14oz canned chopped tomatoes for fresh ones.
– Use curly kale or dark green cabbage instead of cavolo nero.

PROTEIN MAX SALAD BOWL

SERVES: 4 | PREP: 15 MINUTES | COOK: 7 MINUTES

28g
/SERVE

300g/10oz Tenderstem® broccoli, trimmed and each stalk cut in half
2 tbsp sunflower seeds
2 tbsp sesame seeds
100g/3½oz (¾ cup) cashews
4 spring onions (scallions), sliced
225g/8oz (3 cups) frozen edamame beans, defrosted
150g/5oz (2¼ cups) mixed sprouted seeds, e.g. amaranth, alfalfa, broccoli, radish, pea or beansprouts
75g/3oz (½ cup) sun-blush tomatoes in olive oil, drained
1 ripe avocado, peeled, stoned (pitted) and cubed
120g/4oz soft creamy goat's cheese, cut into pieces
1 small bunch of chives, snipped

FOR THE DRESSING:
4 tbsp olive oil
2 tbsp cider vinegar
1 garlic clove, crushed
grated zest and juice of 1 orange
1 tsp clear honey
salt and freshly ground black pepper

This crunchy salad is so healthy and delicious, packed with a nutritional jackpot of protein, vitamins and minerals. The edamame beans, nuts, seeds, cheese and even the broccoli all provide protein. In fact, the process of sprouting helps to boost the protein content of seeds, which also have higher levels of some amino acids.

1 Steam the broccoli in a steamer or a colander covered with a lid placed over a pan of simmering water for 5 minutes or until just tender but still a little crisp.

2 Toast the seeds and cashews in a dry frying pan (skillet) set over a medium heat for 1–2 minutes, tossing gently, until golden brown. Remove and cool.

3 Put the broccoli in a bowl with the spring onions, edamame beans, sprouts, sun-blush tomatoes and avocado. Stir in the toasted seeds and cashews.

4 Make the dressing: blend all the ingredients in a bowl or blitz in a blender.

5 Pour the dressing over the salad and toss gently. Crumble the cheese over the top and serve immediately, sprinkled with chives.

OR YOU CAN TRY THIS...
– Add some fennel, spinach, kale or red or yellow (bell) peppers.
– Try different nuts: walnuts, hazelnuts, pistachios or almonds.
– Sprinkle with pomegranate seeds (arils).
– Vary the beans: try chickpeas, cannellini or butter beans (lima beans).

LIGHT MEALS & SALADS

SPICY SEAFOOD TACOS

SERVES: 4 | PREP: 15 MINUTES | COOK: 10-12 MINUTES

3 tbsp vegetable oil
400g/14oz skinned white
    fish fillets, e.g. cod,
    haddock, sea bass
juice of 1 lime
a handful of coriander
    (cilantro), chopped
200g/7oz large cooked
    peeled prawns (shrimp)
4 large tomatoes
2 red chillies
1 tbsp balsamic vinegar
1 tsp sugar
12 crunchy taco shells
a handful of crisp lettuce
    leaves, e.g. cos (romaine)
    or Little Gem
salt and freshly ground
    black pepper

FOR THE GUACAMOLE:
½ red onion, diced
1 fresh green chilli, diced
1 garlic clove, crushed
½ tsp sea salt crystals
2 ripe medium avocados,
    peeled, stoned (pitted)
    and roughly mashed
1 ripe tomato, deseeded
    and diced
juice of 1 lime
1 small bunch of coriander
    (cilantro), chopped

Tacos make a quick and easy meal, and are so versatile. We've filled these with a mixture of white fish and prawns and added home-made chunky guacamole and spicy tomato purée. The avocados and crunchy tacos contribute to the protein content.

1 Make the guacamole: crush the onion, chilli, garlic and salt using a pestle and mortar. Add the avocados, tomato, lime juice and coriander and mix well.

2 Heat 1 tablespoon of the oil in a large non-stick frying pan (skillet) set over a medium to high heat. Cook the fish fillets for 10–12 minutes, turning halfway, until seared and golden on the outside and cooked through. Cut into chunks and sprinkle with the lime juice and coriander. Add the prawns and season lightly with salt and pepper.

3 Meanwhile, cook the whole tomatoes and chillies in a lightly oiled griddle (grill) pan or under a hot grill until softened and charred. Put them in a blender and blitz with the vinegar, sugar and remaining oil.

4 Fill the tacos with the lettuce, fish and guacamole and drizzle with the puréed tomatoes and chillies.

OR YOU CAN TRY THIS...

– Use salmon fillets instead of white fish and you'll have 37g protein per serving.
– Instead of making the tomato and chilli purée, use ready-made salsa.
– Serve with Greek yoghurt – there's 1g protein in every tablespoon.

TIP: You can warm the taco shells by popping them into a hot oven for 5 minutes.

CHEESY SWEET POTATO JACKETS WITH CHORIZO AND BEAN CHILLI

23g /SERVE

SERVES: 4 | PREP: 10 MINUTES | COOK: 1 HOUR

4 x 200g/7oz sweet potatoes, washed and scrubbed
2 tbsp olive oil
1 onion, finely chopped
2 garlic cloves, crushed
1 red (bell) pepper, deseeded and chopped
1–2 tsp chilli powder
1 x 400g/14oz can (scant 2 cups) chopped tomatoes
1 x 400g/14oz can (2 cups) red kidney beans, rinsed and drained
a few sprigs of coriander (cilantro), chopped
100g/3½oz chorizo, diced
50g/2oz (½ cup) grated Parmesan cheese
salt and freshly ground black pepper

A baked sweet potato makes such an easy meal, and the chorizo and bean chilli takes no time at all to cook – you could even prepare this topping and cook it in advance, then store in a sealed container in the fridge ready to reheat. The beans and spicy chorizo provide the bulk of the protein but there are also significant amounts in the cheese, sweet potatoes, tomatoes and pepper.

1 Preheat the oven to 190°C, 375°F, gas mark 5.

2 Prick the sweet potatoes with a fork and place on a baking tray (cookie sheet). Bake in the oven for 45–50 minutes until tender when you press them gently.

3 Meanwhile, heat the oil in a pan set over a low heat. Cook the onion, garlic and pepper, stirring occasionally, for 6–8 minutes until tender. Stir in the chilli powder and cook for 1 minute. Add the tomatoes and kidney beans and simmer gently for 10–15 minutes until the mixture reduces and thickens. Add the coriander and season to taste.

4 Cook the chorizo in a frying pan (skillet) set over a medium heat for 2–3 minutes, stirring occasionally, until it crisps up and releases its oil. Stir into the bean chilli.

5 Split the baked sweet potatoes in half or cut a cross in the top of each and press gently on the sides to open it up. Spoon the chilli over the top and sprinkle with the grated cheese.

6 Pop back into the hot oven or under a hot grill for 2–3 minutes until melted, bubbling and golden brown.

OR YOU CAN TRY THIS...
– For a veggie option, leave out the chorizo – this will give you 17g protein per serving.

CHILLI PRAWN CAESAR SALAD

SERVES: 4 | PREP: 15 MINUTES | COOK: 15 MINUTES

4 slices stale sourdough
   or country bread
3–4 tbsp olive oil
1 tbsp butter
2 garlic cloves, crushed
juice of 1 lemon
400g/14oz peeled raw large
   tiger prawns (jumbo
   shrimp), frozen and
   defrosted
a handful of flat-leaf parsley,
   finely chopped
a good pinch of crushed
   chilli flakes
2 cos (romaine) lettuces,
   roughly torn into pieces
50g/2oz (½ cup) grated
   Parmesan cheese

Cooking the prawns with garlic, lemon and chilli brings a new dimension to the classic Caesar salad.

1 Preheat the oven to 200°C, 400°F, gas mark 6.

2 Cut the bread into small cubes and toss in 1–2 tablespoons of the olive oil. Spread them out on a baking tray (cookie sheet) and bake in the oven for about 15 minutes until crisp and golden.

3 Meanwhile, make the dressing: put the anchovies, garlic, egg yolks and mustard in a blender or small food processor and blitz to a thick paste. With the motor running, gradually add the oil through the feed tube in a thin steady stream until the dressing is thick and smooth. Stir in the lemon juice and season to taste. If it's too thick, thin it with a little water or lemon juice.

28g
/SERVE

FOR THE DRESSING:
4 anchovies, rinsed
2 garlic cloves, crushed
2 egg yolks
1 tsp Dijon mustard
150ml/5fl oz (generous
    ½ cup) olive oil
juice of ½ lemon
salt and freshly ground
    black pepper

4 Heat the remaining oil and the butter in a frying pan (skillet) set over a medium heat. Cook the garlic for 1 minute without browning. Add the lemon juice and cook for 1–2 minutes until it reduces. Stir in the prawns and cook for 2 minutes each side until they turn pink. Add the parsley and chilli and cook for 2 minutes.

5 Put the lettuce in a salad bowl with the Parmesan and toss gently in most of the dressing. Scatter with the croûtons and arrange the prawns on top. Drizzle with the remaining dressing and serve immediately.

OR YOU CAN TRY THIS...
– Use bought croûtons rather than make them yourself.
– Use mixed lettuce and shredded spinach.
– Fry a diced chilli with the garlic and prawns.

TIP: You can make the dressing by hand – just mash the anchovies, garlic, egg yolks and mustard to a paste and then beat in the oil, a few drops at a time, before adding the lemon juice and seasoning.

MAIN MEALS
(25–50G PROTEIN)

BALSAMIC-GLAZED CHICKEN TRAYBAKE

36g
/SERVE

SERVES: 4 | PREP: 15 MINUTES | COOK: 40-50 MINUTES

3 tbsp olive oil

4 x 125g/4oz chicken breast
   fillets

2 red onions, cut into wedges

600g/1lb 5oz sweet
   potatoes, peeled and
   cut into large chunks

300g/10oz asparagus,
   trimmed

300g/10oz baby plum
   tomatoes

150ml/¼ pint (scant ¾ cup)
   chicken stock

2 tbsp balsamic vinegar

1 tsp thyme leaves

a handful of flat-leaf
   parsley, chopped

sea salt and freshly ground
   black pepper

balsamic glaze, for drizzling

One-pan meals are so easy to make ... and there's minimal washing-up, too. Chicken is a good way of getting lean protein but the sweet potatoes, asparagus and onions are also helpful in increasing the protein content. Serve with some fine green beans or spinach and you'll boost the protein levels even more.

1 Preheat the oven to 190°C, 375°F, gas mark 5.

2 Heat the olive oil in a large roasting tin (pan) set over a medium heat on the hob. Add the chicken and cook for 8–10 minutes, turning occasionally, until browned all over.

3 Add the red onions, sweet potatoes, asparagus and tomatoes. Pour the stock over, sprinkle with the balsamic vinegar and thyme and season with salt and pepper.

4 Roast in the oven for 30–40 minutes until the chicken is cooked through and the vegetables are tender.

5 Serve sprinkled with chopped parsley and drizzled with balsamic glaze.

OR YOU CAN TRY THIS...

– Vary the vegetables – try fennel, aubergine (eggplant), red, green or yellow (bell) peppers, parsnips and baby carrots.
– Sprinkle with oregano or rosemary leaves instead of thyme.
– Drizzle with sweet chilli sauce.

CHEESY STUFFED PORK ROLL

SERVES: 4 | PREP: 15 MINUTES | COOK: 40-45 MINUTES

400g/14oz spinach,
trimmed and washed
50g/2oz sun-blush
tomatoes, chopped
150g/5oz mozzarella,
drained and diced
450g/1lb pork tenderloin
fillet
olive oil, for spraying/
brushing
300g/10oz fine green beans,
trimmed
salt and freshly ground
black pepper
brown rice or baked
potatoes, to serve

Adding this cheesy spinach stuffing makes the pork tenderloin more
succulent as it can become quite dry during cooking. This is quick and
easy to assemble and cook and is full of protein. If you serve it with
nutty, crunchy brown rice or a jacket baked potato you'll add 2.6g
protein per 100g/3½oz serving.

1 Preheat the oven to 190°C, 375°F, gas mark 5.

2 Put the wet spinach in a large pan. Cover and set over a medium
heat. Cook for 2–3 minutes, shaking the pan occasionally, until the
spinach wilts and turns bright green. Drain in a colander, pressing
out any excess liquid with a saucer.

3 Pat dry with kitchen paper (paper towels) and chop roughly. Transfer
to a bowl and mix with the sun-blush tomatoes and mozzarella.

4 Using a sharp knife, cut down through the middle of the pork fillet
lengthways, but not all the way through. Instead of ending up with
2 long pieces you should be able to open it out flat like a book. Place
it between 2 sheets of clingfilm (plastic wrap) or baking parchment
and flatten it out with a mallet or rolling pin.

5 Lay the pork out flat on a clean surface and season lightly with salt
and pepper. Spoon the spinach mixture down the centre and roll up
tightly to enclose the stuffing. Secure with kitchen string. Place in
a roasting tin (pan) and spray or brush lightly with oil. Bake in the
oven for 35–40 minutes until the pork is cooked right through and
no longer pink.

36g
/SERVE

6 Meanwhile, steam the green beans or cook in a pan of lightly salted boiling water until just tender, then drain.

7 Cut the pork into thick slices and serve with the green beans and some brown rice or baked potatoes.

OR YOU CAN TRY THIS...
– Use grated Cheddar cheese instead of mozzarella.
– Add some sage or basil leaves to the stuffing.
– If you can't get sun-blush tomatoes, use sun-dried ones instead.

SUPER PROTEIN BEEF BURRITOS

44g /SERVE

SERVES: 4 | PREP: 15 MINUTES | COOK: 20 MINUTES

2 tbsp oil, plus extra for
    brushing
2 garlic cloves, crushed
500g/1lb 2oz (generous
    2 cups) extra lean minced
    (ground) beef
1–2 tsp chilli powder
1 tsp ground cumin
1 x 400g/14oz can (2 cups)
    black beans, rinsed and
    drained
1 x 200g/7oz can (1 cup)
    chopped tomatoes
a handful of coriander
    (cilantro), finely chopped
juice of 1 lime
2 red onions, thinly sliced
2 red, green or yellow (bell)
    peppers, deseeded and
    thinly sliced
4 large wholewheat tortillas
a few crisp lettuce leaves
100g/3½oz (1 cup) grated
    Cheddar or Monterey
    Jack cheese
salt and freshly ground
    black pepper
guacamole, hot salsa, sour
    cream and salad, to serve

**Use best-quality really lean beef to make these tasty high-protein burritos.
They make an easy family meal and cook in less than 20 minutes.**

1 Heat the oil in a frying pan (skillet) and set over a medium heat.
Cook the garlic for 1 minute without browning. Add the minced
beef and cook, stirring occasionally, for 5 minutes or until browned.
Stir in the chilli powder and cumin.

2 Add the beans and tomatoes and cook for 5 minutes or so until the
beef is cooked and the mixture has reduced. Season to taste with salt
and pepper, and stir in the coriander and lime juice.

3 Meanwhile, lightly oil a griddle (grill) pan and set over a medium
to high heat. Cook the onions and peppers, turning occasionally,
for about 5 minutes until tender and starting to char.

4 Place the tortillas on a clean surface and top with the lettuce and
bean and minced beef mixture. Add the griddled onions and peppers
and roll or fold the tortillas around the filling. Place on a grill (broiler)
pan and sprinkle the cheese over the top. Flash under a hot preheated
grill to melt the cheese.

5 Serve hot with some guacamole, hot salsa, sour cream and some salad.

OR YOU CAN TRY THIS...
– Instead of chilli powder, use diced fresh chillies.
– Drizzle with hot sauce to serve.

STICKY CHICKEN WITH CHICKPEA COUSCOUS

45g
/SERVE

SERVES: 4 | PREP: 15 MINUTES | MARINATE: 15 MINUTES | COOK: 30-40 MINUTES

2 tbsp clear honey
1 tbsp olive oil, plus extra
    for brushing
1 tsp wholegrain mustard
3 garlic cloves, crushed
juice of 1 lemon
4 chicken thighs, bone in,
    skin on
8 chicken wings, bone in,
    skin on
harissa or chilli sauce, to serve

FOR THE CHICKPEA COUSCOUS:

200g/7oz (generous 1 cup)
    couscous (dry weight)
2 tbsp olive oil
grated zest and juice of
    1 lemon
240ml/8fl oz (1 cup) boiling
    chicken stock
200g/7oz (¾ cup) canned
    chickpeas, rinsed and
    drained
skin of 2 preserved lemons,
    diced (pips and flesh
    removed)
50g/2oz (½ cup) toasted
    pine nuts
85g/3oz (½ cup) sultanas
    (golden raisins)
a handful of flat-leaf parsley,
    chopped
salt and freshly ground
    black pepper

This delicious way of serving chicken hits the protein jackpot. The couscous, chickpeas, pine nuts and even the chicken stock all help to increase the protein grams per serving.

1 Preheat the oven to 200°C, 400°F, gas mark 6.

2 In a bowl, mix together the honey, olive oil, mustard, garlic and lemon juice. Add the chicken thighs and wings, turning them in the marinade until coated all over. Cover and chill in the fridge for 15 minutes.

3 Lightly brush a roasting tin (pan) with oil and add the chicken. Cook in the oven for 30–40 minutes, turning and basting occasionally, until cooked right through, sticky and golden brown.

4 Meanwhile, make the couscous: put the couscous, olive oil, lemon zest and juice in a large bowl. Pour in the boiling chicken stock and stir well. Cover the bowl and leave for 10–15 minutes until the couscous has absorbed the liquid. Stir in the chickpeas, preserved lemons, pine nuts, sultanas and parsley. Season to taste with salt and pepper.

5 Serve the chicken with the couscous and some harissa or chilli sauce.

OR YOU CAN TRY THIS...

– Use chopped coriander (cilantro) or mint instead of parsley.
– Stir some diced red onion, chilli and tomatoes into the couscous.
– Use flaked toasted almonds instead of pine nuts.
– Add some sliced pitted olives or diced sun-dried tomatoes to
  the couscous.

SPICY BEEF BROCHETTES WITH MANGO SALSA

30g /SERVE

SERVES: 4 | PREP: 20 MINUTES | COOK: 8-10 MINUTES

500g/1lb 2oz (generous
   2 cups) minced (ground)
   beef (max. 5% fat)
1 red onion, grated
2 garlic cloves, crushed
1 chilli, deseeded and diced
1 tsp ground cumin
1 tsp ground coriander
a handful of coriander
   (cilantro), chopped
vegetable oil, for brushing
   or spraying
1 large red onion, cut into
   rings or wedges
2 red or green (bell)
   peppers, deseeded and
   cut into chunks or rings
300g/10oz (1¾ cups) quinoa
   (uncooked weight)
salt and freshly ground
   black pepper

FOR THE MANGO SALSA:

1 large ripe mango, peeled,
   stoned (pitted) and diced
1 small red onion, diced
3 ripe tomatoes, diced
1 red chilli, diced
1 bunch of coriander
   (cilantro), chopped
juice of 1 lime
sea salt

These brochettes are served with quinoa, which is high in protein, rich in fibre, cholesterol-free and gluten-free. If wished, you can cook them over hot coals on a barbecue and enjoy the smoky flavour and aroma.

1 Make the mango salsa: mix all the ingredients together and season to taste.

2 Mix together the minced beef, grated onion, garlic, chilli, ground spices and coriander in a bowl with some salt and pepper. Using your hands, mould the mixture into 12 cylindrical sausage shapes. Thread them onto skewers (see tip) and brush or spray lightly with oil.

3 Place on a foil-lined grill (broiler) pan with the onion rings or wedges and the peppers. Cook under a hot grill, turning occasionally, for 8–10 minutes until the beef is browned and slightly charred and the vegetables are just tender.

4 Meanwhile, cook the quinoa according to the instructions on the packet.

5 Serve hot with the quinoa and mango salsa.

OR YOU CAN TRY THIS...

– Use minced lamb instead of beef.
– Crunchy nutty brown rice can be substituted for the quinoa.
– Instead of mango salsa, serve with spicy mango chutney and some cooling plain yoghurt.

TIP: You can use wooden or metal skewers. If using wooden ones, soak them in water first for 10 minutes to prevent them burning.

SALMON AND SPINACH ROULADE

SERVES: 4 | PREP: 20 MINUTES | CHILL: 2 HOURS | COOK: 25 MINUTES

butter, for greasing
500g/1lb 2oz spinach,
    trimmed and washed
3 medium free-range eggs,
    separated
225g/8oz (generous 1 cup)
    cream cheese
200g/7oz smoked salmon,
    chopped
1 bunch of chives, chopped
grated zest of 1 lemon

FOR THE WHITE SAUCE:
75g/3oz (scant ½ cup)
    butter
50g/2oz (½ cup) plain (all-
    purpose) flour
600ml/1 pint (2½ cups)
    milk
a pinch of ground nutmeg
salt and freshly ground
    black pepper

We've used smoked salmon to make this green-flecked roulade but it's also a great way to use up leftover cooked salmon. Spinach is not only rich in protein but also a good source of iron, calcium, folate and other minerals and vitamins, making it a good choice for pregnant women and nursing mothers as well as athletes and older people.

1 Preheat the oven to 190°C, 375°F, gas mark 5. Lightly grease a 20 x 30cm (8 x 12in) Swiss roll tin (jelly roll pan) with baking parchment.

2 Make the white sauce: melt the butter in a non-stick pan set over a low heat and stir in the flour with a wooden spoon. Cook for 2 minutes until it smells biscuity and then add the milk, a little at a time, stirring or whisking until smooth. Keep stirring over a low heat until the sauce thickens. Remove from the heat and season with the nutmeg, salt and pepper, then pour into a food processor.

3 Meanwhile, put the wet spinach in a large pan and place over a medium heat. Cover the pan and cook for about 2 minutes, shaking the pan occasionally, until the leaves turn bright green and wilt. Drain in a colander, pressing down with a saucer to squeeze out any moisture.

4 Add the spinach to the food processor and pulse briefly with the white sauce. Add the egg yolks and blitz until well blended. Transfer to a large bowl.

5 In a clean, dry bowl, beat the egg whites until they form soft peaks. Using a metal spoon, fold gently into the spinach mixture in a figure-of-eight motion. Spoon into the prepared tin and cook in the oven for 15 minutes or until the roulade is well-risen and springs back when lightly pressed with a finger. Leave to cool in the tin.

6 Mix the cream cheese with the smoked salmon, chives and lemon zest.

7 Invert the cold spinach roulade onto a large sheet of baking parchment and peel away the backing paper as you remove the tin. Spread the cheese and smoked salmon mixture over the roulade but not quite up to the edges.

8 Roll up the roulade, using the baking parchment underneath to help you. Place on a serving plate, seam-side down, then cover and chill in the fridge for at least 2 hours before cutting into slices to serve.

OR YOU CAN TRY THIS...
- Mix the cooked spinach with some watercress or rocket (arugula).
- Use smoked salmon trimmings – they are cheaper than slices.
- Vary the herbs: try dill, parsley or tarragon.
- Use ricotta instead of cream cheese and you will increase the protein per serving by 1.3g.

CHICKEN MILANESE

SERVES: 4 | PREP: 20 MINUTES | DRAIN: 30 MINUTES | COOK: 15 MINUTES

4 x 125g/4oz skinless
  chicken breast fillets
plain (all-purpose) flour,
  for dusting
2 medium free-range
  eggs, beaten
90g/3½oz (1 cup) dried
  breadcrumbs
75g/3oz (¾ cup) grated
  Parmesan cheese
4 tbsp olive oil
15g/½oz butter
400g/14oz spaghetti
  (dry weight)
salt and freshly ground
  black pepper

**FOR THE FRESH TOMATO
  SAUCE:**
900g/2lb ripe tomatoes
1 garlic clove, crushed
1 tsp sugar
a handful of basil leaves,
  chopped
120ml/4fl oz (½ cup)
  fruity green olive oil
1 tbsp red wine vinegar

**This classic Italian dish is not only simple and delicious but also packed
with protein. Serving the crisp, golden-brown chicken escalopes with pasta
and cheese boosts the protein content to make a very sustaining meal.**

1 Make the fresh tomato sauce: prick the tomatoes a few times with a
  knife and place them in a large bowl. Pour boiling water over the top,
  leave for 30 seconds and then drain. Peel off the skins and cut each
  one in half.

2 Scoop out the seeds and place the tomatoes, cut-side down, on some
  kitchen paper (paper towels). Leave to drain for 30 minutes, then
  chop them into small pieces and place in a bowl with the garlic,
  sugar, basil, olive oil and vinegar. Mix well and season to taste with
  salt and pepper. Set aside while you cook the chicken and pasta.

3 Cut each chicken breast in half horizontally. Place it between 2 sheets
  of greaseproof paper or clingfilm (plastic wrap) and flatten with a mallet
  or a rolling pin until it is 5mm/¼in thick. Place the flour, beaten eggs
  and the breadcrumbs mixed with 4 tablespoons of the grated Parmesan
  onto 3 separate plates. Dust the chicken escalopes lightly with flour
  on both sides, one at a time, dip each into the beaten egg, shaking off
  the excess, then coat in the cheesy breadcrumbs on both sides.

4 Heat the oil and butter in a large frying pan (skillet) set over a medium
  to high heat. When it's hot, add the breadcrumbed chicken, in batches,
  and cook for 3–4 minutes each side until cooked right through and
  golden brown and crisp. Remove to a plate lined with kitchen paper.

5 Meanwhile, cook the spaghetti according to the instructions on the
  packet and drain well. Return to the hot pan and toss with the fresh
  tomato sauce to coat.

6 Serve the hot chicken with the pasta, sprinkled with the remaining
  Parmesan.

CHEESY BEAN AND MUSHROOM BAKE

SERVES: 4 | PREP: 15 MINUTES | COOK: 45-55 MINUTES

31g
/SERVE

3 tbsp olive oil, plus extra
    for drizzling
1 large onion, chopped
2 garlic cloves, crushed
500g/1lb 2oz chestnut or
    white mushrooms, sliced
2 x 400g/14oz cans (4 cups)
    cannellini beans, rinsed
    and drained
100g/3½oz baby spinach
    leaves
a handful of flat-leaf parsley,
    finely chopped
50g/2oz (1 cup) fresh
    wholemeal breadcrumbs
100g/3½oz (1 cup) grated
    Cheddar cheese

FOR THE WHITE SAUCE:
60g/2oz (¼ cup) butter
60g/2oz (generous ½ cup)
    plain (all-purpose) flour
600ml/1 pint (2½ cups) milk
a pinch of ground nutmeg
salt and freshly ground
    black pepper

TIP: This is delicious
served with steamed
green vegetables or a
crisp salad.

This is real comfort food for a cold autumnal or winter's night. It's also simple to make and very economical. Beans are a good source of vegetable protein but they can't provide all the essential amino acids you need, so it's best to eat this with some protein-rich brown rice, buckwheat or quinoa.

1 Preheat the oven to 180°C, 350°F, gas mark 4.

2 Heat the oil in a pan set over a low heat. Add the onion and garlic and cook for 6–8 minutes, stirring occasionally, until softened but not coloured. Add the mushrooms and cook, stirring occasionally, for 5 minutes or until tender and golden.

3 Meanwhile, make the white sauce: melt the butter in a non-stick pan set over a low heat and stir in the flour with a wooden spoon. Cook for 2 minutes until it smells biscuity and then add the milk, a little at a time, stirring or whisking until smooth. Keep stirring over a low heat until the sauce thickens. Remove from the heat and season with the nutmeg, salt and pepper.

4 Add the beans, spinach, parsley and white sauce to the onion and mushroom mixture and stir gently. Transfer to a baking dish.

5 Sprinkle the breadcrumbs and cheese over the top and drizzle with a little oil. Bake in the oven for 30–40 minutes until crisp and golden brown and the sauce is bubbling up around the edges. Serve hot.

OR YOU CAN TRY THIS...
– Use grated Parmesan, Gruyère, Emmental or pecorino cheese.
– Substitute butter beans (lima beans) or haricot beans for cannellini.
– Instead of parsley, try chopped chives or dill.
– Add chopped fennel bulb, leeks, courgettes (zucchini) or cherry tomatoes.

SPAGHETTI CARBONARA

SERVES: 4 | PREP: 10 MINUTES | COOK: 10 MINUTES

27g
/SERVE

1 tbsp olive oil
2 garlic cloves, thinly sliced
150g/5oz pancetta or bacon, cubed
30g/1oz (2 tbsp) butter
2 large eggs and 2 egg yolks
60ml/2fl oz (¼ cup) crème fraîche
100g/3½oz (scant 1 cup) grated Parmesan cheese, plus extra to serve
500g/1lb 2oz spaghetti (dry weight)
a handful of flat-leaf parsley, finely chopped
salt and freshly ground black pepper

This classic Roman way of serving pasta is really quick and easy to prepare and cook. Although it's soothing and creamy, it still packs quite a protein punch. Because raw eggs are stirred into the spaghetti, pregnant women should take care to cook them thoroughly and not eat this if they are still runny.

1 Heat the oil in a pan set over a low to medium heat and cook the garlic for a couple of minutes until it colours. Remove immediately and discard. Add the pancetta or bacon to the pan and cook for about 5 minutes, turning occasionally, until crispy, golden and most of the fat has run out. Remove from the heat.

2 In a bowl, beat together the eggs, yolks, crème fraîche and Parmesan. Add a good grinding of black pepper.

3 Meanwhile, cook the spaghetti according to the instructions on the packet until it's al dente (tender but still slightly firm).

4 Drain the pasta, reserving a ladleful of the cooking water, and add the pasta to the pan containing the bacon or pancetta. Stir in the egg and cheese mixture. Off the heat, keep stirring and tossing the pasta until the egg mixture thickens and is creamy. If it's too thick, you can thin it with some of the reserved pasta cooking liquid. Check the seasoning, adding salt if required.

5 Divide the pasta between 4 warm shallow serving bowls. Serve hot, sprinkled with parsley and more Parmesan.

OR YOU CAN TRY THIS...
– Use double (heavy) cream instead of crème fraîche.
– Use grated pecorino instead of Parmesan, or a mixture of both.
– For a vegetarian carbonara, use spinach, peas and fried mushrooms instead of bacon.

TIP: This is a delicious way of using up leftover cooked ham – cut it into dice and substitute it for the pancetta or bacon.

DHAL WITH SPICY SEEDY TOPPING

SERVES: 4 | PREP: 15 MINUTES | COOK: 35-40 MINUTES

3 tbsp vegetable oil
2 garlic cloves, crushed
1 tsp grated fresh root ginger
1 green chilli, finely diced
1 tsp black mustard seeds
2 tsp ground turmeric
1 tsp garam masala
300g/10oz (1½ cups) split
  red lentils
600ml/1 pint (2½ cups) hot
  vegetable stock
400ml/14fl oz (scant 1¾
  cups) canned coconut milk
4 ripe tomatoes, roughly
  chopped
1 x 400g/14oz can (2 cups)
  chickpeas, rinsed
  and drained
200g/7oz baby spinach leaves
juice of 1 lime
400g/14oz sweet potatoes,
  sliced (skin left on)
a handful of coriander
  (cilantro), chopped
4 naan breads, warmed,
  to serve

A bowl of steaming spicy dhal is always warming and sustaining. The combination of lentils, which are a good source of vegetarian slow-release protein and carbohydrate, and starchy sweet potatoes is a great one. Not only do they taste good but they're also rich in dietary fibre, essential vitamins and minerals.

1 Heat 2 tablespoons of the oil in a large pan set over a low to medium heat, add the garlic, ginger and chilli and cook for 2 minutes without colouring. Stir in the mustard seeds and ground spices and when the seeds start to pop, add the lentils, stock and coconut milk. Bring to the boil, then reduce the heat and simmer gently for 15 minutes.

2 Add the tomatoes and chickpeas and simmer for 15–20 minutes until the dhal is thick and creamy. If it's still a bit liquid, cook for a little longer; if it's too thick, thin it with some more stock. Stir in the spinach and lime juice and check the seasoning.

3 Meanwhile, make the spicy seedy topping: heat the oil in a frying pan (skillet) set over a medium heat and cook the onion, stirring occasionally, until it starts to caramelise and turn golden brown. Add the garlic, chilli, seeds and curry leaves and cook for 2 minutes. Season lightly with salt and pepper.

4 When the dhal is nearly ready, put the sweet potato slices with the remaining oil in a bowl and toss gently. Set a griddle (grill) pan over a medium heat and when it's really hot add the sweet potato. Cook for 2–3 minutes each side until tender and slightly charred.

25g
/SERVE

**FOR THE SPICY SEEDY
  TOPPING:**
2 tbsp rapeseed oil
1 large onion, thinly sliced
2 garlic cloves, thinly sliced
1 red chilli, deseeded and
  shredded
1 tsp cumin seeds
1 tsp yellow mustard seeds
8 fresh curry leaves
salt and freshly ground
  black pepper

5 Divide the dhal between 4 shallow bowls and top with the sweet
  potato slices and the spicy seedy topping. Scatter some coriander
  over the top and serve with warm naan bread.

OR YOU CAN TRY THIS...
– Vary the spices in the dhal: try ground cinnamon, cumin, fennel,
  cardamom or coriander seeds.
– Use griddled pumpkin or squash instead of sweet potato.

JAMAICAN JERK PRAWNS

SERVES: 4 | PREP: 20 MINUTES | CHILL: 30 MINUTES | COOK: 20 MINUTES

28g
/SERVE

500g/1lb 2oz large raw shelled
  prawns (jumbo shrimp)
200g/7oz (generous 1 cup)
  quinoa (raw weight)
500ml/17fl oz (generous
  2 cups) vegetable stock
4 tbsp olive oil
1 bunch of spring onions
  (scallions), thinly sliced
a handful of coriander
  (cilantro), chopped
1 small ripe mango, peeled,
  stoned (pitted) and diced
1 large ripe avocado, peeled,
  stoned (pitted) and diced
juice of 2 limes
salt and freshly ground
  black pepper

FOR THE JERK PASTE:
2 tsp allspice berries
2 tsp black peppercorns
1 shallot, finely chopped
2 garlic cloves, crushed
2.5cm/1in piece fresh root
  ginger, peeled and diced
2 chillies, diced
½ tsp ground cinnamon
a pinch of ground nutmeg
leaves stripped from 4 sprigs
  of thyme
2 tsp brown sugar
1 tbsp soy sauce
juice of 1 lime

If you use Scotch bonnet chillies in the jerk paste it will be really fiery
and authentic. Many supermarkets and delicatessens stock them, and
they are also available online. Quinoa tastes quite bland, so it's best
cooked in some flavoursome stock, preferably home-made or fresh,
rather than using bouillon cubes.

1 Make the jerk paste: crush the allspice berries and peppercorns
  in a pestle and mortar. Put them in a blender with all the other
  ingredients and blitz to a paste. Transfer to a bowl and add the
  prawns. Stir gently until coated. Cover and leave in the fridge for
  at least 30 minutes.

2 Rinse the quinoa under running cold water, then drain. Bring the stock
  to the boil and tip in the quinoa. Reduce the heat, cover the pan and
  simmer gently for 15 minutes or until tender and most of the stock has
  been absorbed. Turn off the heat and leave to steam in the pan for
  6–8 minutes before draining off any excess liquid. Fluff up with a fork.

3 Stir 2 tablespoons of the olive oil, the spring onions, coriander, mango,
  avocado and lime juice into the quinoa. Season to taste with salt and
  pepper. Cover and set aside.

4 Heat the remaining oil in a frying pan (skillet) or a griddle (grill)
  pan set over a medium to high heat. Add the prawns and cook for
  1–2 minutes each side until they turn pink.

5 Divide the quinoa between 4 serving plates and arrange the prawns
  on top. Serve immediately.

OR YOU CAN TRY THIS...
– Use chicken, firm white fish or salmon instead of prawns.
– Stir some pomegranate seeds (arils), diced papaya (pawpaw),
  chopped spinach or cherry tomatoes into the quinoa.
– Use lemon instead of lime juice in the marinade.

CHEESY MACARONI AND BROCCOLI BAKE

28g
/SERVE

SERVES: 4 | PREP: 15 MINUTES | COOK: 30-35 MINUTES

300g/10oz (3 cups)
 macaroni (dry weight)
400g/14oz broccoli,
 separated into florets
50g/2oz (½ cup) grated
 Cheddar cheese
50g/2oz (scant ½ cup)
 chopped walnuts
50g/2oz (1 cup) fresh
 wholemeal breadcrumbs
olive oil, for drizzling
grilled (broiled) tomatoes
 and salad, to serve

FOR THE WHITE SAUCE:
75g/3oz (scant ½ cup)
 butter
50g/2oz (½ cup) plain
 (all-purpose) flour
600ml/1 pint (2½ cups)
 milk
75g/3oz (¾ cup) grated
 Cheddar cheese
2 tsp Dijon mustard
salt and freshly ground
 black pepper

This delicious homely bake is real comfort food – pasta in a creamy sauce with a crunchy cheesy topping. Broccoli is a good source of plant protein and it also contains vitamin C, zinc and lutein, which help protect your skin and keep it healthy, especially in cold weather.

1 Preheat the oven to 190°C, 375°F, gas mark 5.

2 Cook the macaroni in a large pan of lightly salted boiling water according to the packet instructions. Drain and keep warm.

3 Cook the broccoli in a pan of boiling salted water or in a steamer or colander placed over the cooking macaroni for about 5 minutes until just tender but not mushy. Drain well.

4 Meanwhile, make the white sauce: melt the butter in a non-stick pan set over a low heat and stir in the flour with a wooden spoon. Cook for 2 minutes until it smells biscuity and then add the milk, a little at a time, stirring or whisking until smooth. Keep stirring over a low heat until the sauce thickens. Stir in the cheese and mustard and cook for 1 minute. Season with salt and pepper.

5 Put the macaroni and broccoli in a large ovenproof dish. Pour the sauce over the top and sprinkle with the grated cheese, walnuts and breadcrumbs. Drizzle with some olive oil.

6 Bake in the oven for 20–25 minutes until bubbling, crisp and golden brown. Serve with some grilled (broiled) tomatoes and salad.

OR YOU CAN TRY THIS...
– Use cauliflower instead of broccoli, or a mixture of both.
– Instead of Cheddar, try Parmesan, Gruyère or even some crumbled blue cheese.
– Add some cooked mushrooms or leeks.

SPICY SALMON AND BROCCOLI TRAYBAKE

SERVES: 4 | PREP: 10 MINUTES | MARINATE: 15 MINUTES | COOK: 20 MINUTES

44g
/SERVE

2 tbsp teriyaki or light
   soy sauce
juice of 1 small lime
a pinch of sugar
4 x 150g/5oz skinned
   salmon fillets
400g/14oz Tenderstem®
   broccoli, trimmed
2 tbsp light olive oil
250g/9oz cherry tomatoes
   on the vine
300g/10oz brown rice
   (dry weight)
salt and freshly ground
   black pepper

FOR THE DRESSING:

2 tbsp teriyaki or light
   soy sauce
2 tbsp light olive oil
1 tsp sesame oil
juice of 1 lime
1 red bird's eye chilli,
   shredded
1 tsp grated fresh root
   ginger

One-pan meals are so simple to prepare – just throw everything into the pan then sit back and relax. Salmon is not only one of the best sources of protein but it is also rich in omega-3 oils that help protect your heart.

1 Preheat the oven to 180°C, 350°F, gas mark 4.

2 Mix together the teriyaki or soy sauce, lime juice and sugar. Pour over the salmon in a bowl and leave in a cool place for 15 minutes.

3 In a large roasting tin (pan), toss the broccoli in the olive oil. Add the salmon and cook in the oven for 15 minutes. Add the tomatoes and return to the oven for a further 5 minutes.

4 Meanwhile, cook the rice according to the instructions on the packet.

5 Mix all the dressing ingredients together and drizzle over the cooked salmon, broccoli and tomatoes. Check the seasoning and serve immediately with the cooked rice.

OR YOU CAN TRY THIS...

– Use calabrese or cauliflower and cut into florets.
– Add some courgettes (zucchini), red onions or (bell) peppers.
– Sprinkle with chopped coriander (cilantro) or dill.
– Substitute lemon juice for lime.
– Serve with egg noodles instead of rice.

VEGAN ENCHILADAS

SERVES: 4 | PREP: 20 MINUTES | COOK: 40 MINUTES

27g
/SERVE

3 tbsp olive oil
1 red onion, diced
2 garlic cloves, crushed
1 red chilli, diced
600g/1lb 5oz sweet potatoes,
    peeled and cut into cubes
½ tsp ground cumin
½ tsp ground cinnamon
2 x 400g/14oz cans (4 cups)
    red kidney beans, rinsed
    and drained
200g/7oz (scant 1 cup)
    canned sweetcorn kernels
    in water, drained
juice of 1 lime
1 bunch of coriander
    (cilantro), chopped
1 tsp chilli powder
1 x 400g/14oz can (2 cups)
    chopped tomatoes
a pinch of sugar
8 small wholewheat tortillas
50g/2oz (½ cup) grated
    dairy-free vegan cheese
100ml/3½fl oz (scant ½ cup)
    dairy-free vegan sour
    cream
guacamole and salad,
    to serve

These spicy enchiladas provide plant protein from a variety of sources, including beans, sweet potatoes, sweetcorn, tomatoes, tortillas and a vegan alternative to sour cream. For a more authentic flavour use Mexican jalapeño or habanero chillies, if you can get them, and add some smoky chipotle spice to the filling or the sauce. You can buy dairy-free vegan cheese in most health food stores and supermarkets.

1 Preheat the oven to 200°C, 400°F, gas mark 6.

2 Make the filling: heat 2 tablespoons of the oil in a frying pan (skillet) set over a medium heat. Cook the onion, 1 garlic clove and the chilli for 5 minutes. Add the sweet potatoes and stir in the ground spices. Cook for 6–8 minutes, stirring occasionally, until tender and golden brown. Add the kidney beans and sweetcorn and heat through gently. Stir in the lime juice and half the coriander. Season to taste.

3 Meanwhile, make the sauce: heat the remaining oil in a pan set over a low heat and cook the remaining garlic clove for 1 minute without browning. Stir in the chilli powder and add the tomatoes and sugar. Increase the heat and cook, stirring occasionally, for 5 minutes or so until it reduces and thickens. Add the remaining coriander and season to taste, then blitz in a blender or food processor until smooth.

4 Divide the filling between the tortillas and roll them up. Place them, seam-side down, in a large ovenproof dish and pour the sauce over the top. Sprinkle with the grated cheese.

5 Cover with foil and bake in the oven for 20 minutes. Uncover and bake for 5 minutes until the cheese has browned.

6 Serve hot, topped with the sour cream and guacamole, with salad.

OR YOU CAN TRY THIS...
– Use black beans instead of red.
– Add diced red (bell) peppers and mushrooms to the filling.

PROTEIN POWDER

NOTE: The amount of protein in protein powder can vary between different brands. The quantities in this section are calculated from an average of 75g of protein per 100g of powder.

HIGH-PROTEIN BREAKFAST PANCAKES

SERVES: 2 | PREP: 10 MINUTES | COOK: 20 MINUTES*

33g
/SERVE

50g/2oz (scant 4 tbsp)
vanilla protein powder
1 tsp baking powder
90ml/3fl oz (generous
¼ cup) unsweetened
almond milk
1 large free-range egg
1 tbsp chia seeds
1 tbsp vegetable oil
4 rashers (slices) lean
back bacon
maple syrup, for drizzling
1 ripe medium avocado,
peeled, stoned (pitted)
and sliced

These nutritious pancakes are packed with protein and so easy to make. They are a healthy and delicious way to kick-start your day. This recipe makes 6–8 pancakes.

1 Make the pancake batter: blitz the protein powder, baking powder, milk, egg and seeds in a blender until smooth. Transfer to a jug or bowl.

2 Heat a little of the oil in a non-stick frying pan (skillet) set over a medium heat. Add a small amount of the pancake batter and cook for 2 minutes or until golden brown and set underneath. Flip it over and cook the other side.

3 Remove from the pan and drain on kitchen paper (paper towels). Keep warm while you cook the rest of the pancakes.

4 Meanwhile, grill (broil) or fry the bacon until crisp and golden brown.

5 Serve the hot pancakes, drizzled with maple syrup, with the bacon and avocado.

OR YOU CAN TRY THIS...
– Serve the pancakes with some sliced banana and a dollop of thick Greek yoghurt or cream cheese.
– Use chocolate or strawberry protein powder instead of vanilla.
– Vary the seeds or add a good pinch of ground cinnamon.
– Add a handful of blueberries to the batter before cooking.
– Use soya milk instead of almond milk and you will add 1.5g protein per serving.
– Use coconut oil instead of vegetable oil.
– Drizzle with clear honey or agave syrup.

* less if you use a large pan and cook more than one at a time

TIP: You can make the batter in advance and store in an airtight container in the fridge until you're ready to cook the pancakes, where it will last for up to 3 days.

SUPER GREEN SMOOTHIE

SERVES: 1 | PREP: 10 MINUTES

43g
/SERVE

50g/2oz kale or leaf spinach,
    washed and trimmed
25g/1oz (2 tbsp) vanilla
    protein powder
25g/1oz (scant ¼ cup)
    blanched almonds
1 tbsp chia seeds
1 tbsp hemp seeds
1 ripe banana, frozen
300ml/½ pint (1¼ cups)
    unsweetened soya milk

Unlike many smoothies, this dairy-free version is low in sugar and high in protein and plant fibre, making it a great way to start your day. It helps you to stay focused, stabilises blood sugar levels and curbs your appetite so you're less likely to snack. It's the perfect go-to breakfast.

1 Blitz all the ingredients in a blender until really smooth. This may take up to 2 minutes.

2 Pour into a tall glass and drink immediately.

OR YOU CAN TRY THIS...
– Instead of vanilla protein powder, try chocolate.
– Vary the seeds – try pumpkin or flaxseeds.
– Use almond, oat, rice or coconut milk – or dairy milk.
– For convenience, you could use baby spinach leaves.
– Add some chopped mango or apple for sweetness.

TIP: Depending on whether you like your smoothie thick or more liquid, you can just add extra fruit and vegetables or more milk until you have the desired consistency.

PROTEIN POWDER

CHOCOLATE PROTEIN PORRIDGE BOWL

SERVES: 2 | PREP: 5 MINUTES | COOK: 10 MINUTES

33g /SERVE

100g/3½oz (scant 1 cup)
    rolled oats
a pinch of salt
600ml/1 pint (2½ cups)
    almond milk
50g/2oz (4 tbsp) chocolate
    protein powder
2 tbsp peanut butter
2 tsp maple syrup (optional)
15g/1oz (scant ¼ cup) dark
    (bittersweet) chocolate,
    coarsely grated
100g/3½oz (1 cup)
    raspberries
4 tbsp Greek yoghurt

Porridge oats are the perfect breakfast as they are low GI (glycaemic index), releasing energy slowly and gradually throughout the morning to keep your blood sugar levels balanced and prevent sugar highs. You'll have more stamina and feel full for longer.

1 Put the rolled oats, salt and milk in a non-stick pan. Stir with a wooden spoon over a low to medium heat until the porridge starts to thicken. Reduce the heat to a bare simmer and cook gently until the porridge is smooth, thick and creamy. If it's too thick, just add a little water or more milk.

2 Stir in the protein powder until completely dissolved and then swirl in the peanut butter. Divide between 2 serving bowls.

3 Drizzle with maple syrup (if using) and sprinkle with the grated chocolate and raspberries. Serve immediately with the yoghurt.

OR YOU CAN TRY THIS...
– Stir the grated chocolate into the porridge instead of sprinkling over the top.
– Top with blueberries, strawberries or sliced banana.
– Sprinkle some chopped walnuts or almonds over the porridge.
– Use cashew or almond butter instead of peanut butter.
– Sprinkle with cacao nibs.

TIP: This porridge keeps well, so you can put some in a sealed container in the fridge and reheat it the following day in the microwave.

CHIA SEED PROTEIN POWER POTS

30g /SERVE

SERVES: 2 | PREP: 10 MINUTES | CHILL: OVERNIGHT

1 large banana, mashed
2 tsp cashew or almond
   butter
50g/2oz (scant 4 tbsp)
   vanilla protein powder
300ml/½ pint (1¼ cups)
   unsweetened almond
   milk
a few drops of vanilla
   extract
6 tbsp chia seeds
100g/3½oz (scant 1 cup)
   raspberries
2 tbsp coconut flakes
2 tbsp chopped walnuts
maple syrup or clear honey,
   for drizzling

Chia seeds make a delicious 'porridge', which is so quick and simple to prepare. When added to a liquid they swell and thicken it – they have the ability to absorb approximately ten times their dry weight. Packed with nutrients, they are a rich source of protein, with 2g for every tablespoon.

1 Put the mashed banana, nut butter, protein powder, milk and vanilla extract in a blender and blitz until smooth.

2 Transfer to a bowl and stir in the chia seeds, distributing them evenly throughout the mixture – it should start thickening immediately. Pour into 2 screwtop glass jars and cover with the lids or some clingfilm (plastic wrap). Leave to chill overnight in the fridge.

3 The mixture should be set by the following morning. Just before serving, top with the berries, coconut flakes and walnuts and drizzle with maple syrup or honey.

OR YOU CAN TRY THIS...
– Top with blueberries or chopped apricots, peaches, nectarines or mango.
– Use chocolate or strawberry protein powder.
– Use soya or coconut milk.

TIP: Eat for breakfast or take the pots to work with you for a high-protein snack or packed lunch.

PROTEIN POWDER

CHOC CHIP PROTEIN COOKIES

MAKES: 20 | PREP: 15 MINUTES | CHILL: 30 MINUTES | COOK: 12-15 MINUTES

7g /COOKIE

100g/3½oz (generous ½ cup) butter

100g/3½oz (½ cup) peanut butter

200g/7oz (1 cup) soft brown sugar

2 medium free-range eggs, beaten

a few drops of vanilla extract

150g/5oz (1¼ cups) plain (all-purpose) flour

75g/3oz (1 cup) vanilla protein powder

½ tsp baking powder

½ tsp bicarbonate of soda (baking soda)

50g/2oz chopped salted peanuts

100g/3½oz (scant 1 cup) dark (bittersweet) chocolate chips

TIP: If the mixture is too dry to form a soft dough, moisten it with a little milk.

You can boost the protein content of many baked cakes, cookies and bread loaves by substituting protein powder for up to one-third of the flour. The peanuts, eggs, nut butter, flour and chocolate all contribute to the protein count.

1 Using a food mixer or hand-held electric whisk, beat the butter, peanut butter and sugar together until light, fluffy and creamy. Beat in the eggs and vanilla extract. Add the flour, protein powder, baking powder and bicarbonate of soda and beat well. Stir in the peanuts and chocolate chips.

2 Form the dough into a ball and cover with clingfilm (plastic wrap). Leave to chill in the fridge for at least 30 minutes.

3 Preheat the oven to 180°C, 350°F, gas mark 4. Line 2 baking trays (cookie sheets) with baking parchment.

4 Take small portions of the dough – about the size of a heaped teaspoon – and roll each one into a ball. Arrange them in rows on the lined baking trays, leaving some space around them to expand on cooking. Press down lightly with a fork to flatten them.

5 Bake in the oven for 12–15 minutes until cooked, golden brown and slightly firm to the touch. Cool on a wire rack and store in an airtight tin for up to 1 week.

OR YOU CAN TRY THIS...
– Use almond butter and chopped almonds.
– Substitute chocolate protein powder for vanilla.

SEEDY PROTEIN LOAF

MAKES: 1 LOAF (16 SLICES) | PREP: 15 MINUTES | STAND: 30 MINUTES | COOK: 1–1¼ HOURS

175g/6oz (1¾ cups)
  wholewheat flour
100g/3½oz (generous 1 cup)
  rolled oats
75g/3oz (1 cup)
  protein powder
50g/2oz (scant ½ cup)
  ground flaxseed
¼ tsp sea salt
100g/3½oz (1 cup) mixed
  seeds, e.g. linseeds,
  pumpkin, sunflower,
  cumin
4 tbsp sesame seeds
1 tsp ground cinnamon
½ tsp grated nutmeg
100g/3½oz (scant ¾ cup)
  raisins
100g/3½oz (generous
  ½ cup) chopped dates
50g/2oz (½ cup) chopped
  hazelnuts, plus extra for
  sprinkling
300ml/½ pint (1¼ cups)
  unsweetened almond
  milk
2 medium free-range eggs
1 tbsp malt extract

This protein-packed, high-fibre loaf is really healthy, and because there's no yeast, there's no kneading and rising and it's easy to make. Serve it with cheese and add more protein grams.

1 In a large mixing bowl, mix together the flour, oats, protein powder, ground flaxseed and salt. Stir in the seeds, ground spices, raisins, dates and nuts to evenly combine, then make a well in the centre of the dry mixture.

2 In another bowl beat together the milk, eggs and malt extract until well combined. Pour this mixture into the well in the dry ingredients and stir in until everything is combined and smooth. If the mixture is too stiff and not dropping off the spoon, just add a little extra milk to loosen it. Leave to stand at room temperature for 30 minutes.

3 Preheat the oven to 190°C, 375°F, gas mark 5. Lightly oil a 500g/1lb 2oz loaf tin (pan) and line with baking parchment.

4 Transfer the mixture to the prepared loaf tin. Bake in the oven for 1–1¼ hours or until the loaf is cooked right through. It's ready when a skewer inserted in the middle comes out clean.

5 Cool in the tin, then turn out onto a wire rack to cool completely. Serve the loaf cut into slices. This will keep well for 3–4 days if wrapped in foil.

OR YOU CAN TRY THIS...
- Add some caraway, fennel or nigella seeds.
- Add some ground ginger or a pinch of allspice.
- Try chopped walnuts, pecans, pistachios or almonds instead of hazelnuts.

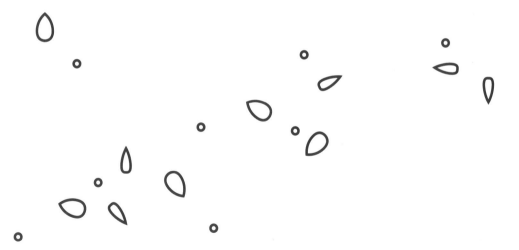

BLUEBERRY PROTEIN MUFFINS

MAKES: 12 | PREP: 15 MINUTES | COOK: 20 MINUTES

9.5g /MUFFIN

100g/3½oz (½ cup) butter, softened
150g/5oz (generous ½ cup) golden caster (superfine) sugar
2 large free-range eggs
150g/5oz (generous ½ cup) Greek yoghurt
3 tbsp milk
a few drops of vanilla extract
75g/3oz (1 cup) vanilla protein powder
175g/6oz (1½ cups) plain (all-purpose) flour
2 tsp baking powder
1 tsp bicarbonate of soda (baking soda)
¼ tsp salt
2 tbsp chia seeds
3 tbsp poppy seeds
100g/3½oz (1 cup) fresh blueberries

Everybody loves blueberry muffins. You can eat them as a snack, a teatime treat or for breakfast and brunch. Adding protein powder to this recipe doubles the protein content of each muffin. We've used vanilla-flavoured powder but you could swap it for a chocolate one.

1 Preheat the oven to 180°C, 350°F, gas mark 4. Line a 12-hole muffin tin (pan) with paper cases (liners).

2 Beat the butter and sugar together in a food mixer or with an electric hand-held whisk until light and fluffy.

3 Beat in the eggs, one at a time – don't worry if the mixture curdles. Beat in the yoghurt, milk and vanilla extract.

4 Put the protein powder in a bowl and sift in the flour, baking powder and bicarbonate of soda. Stir in the salt and seeds. Fold these dry ingredients into the yoghurt mixture. You want to end up with a mixture that is neither too stiff nor too liquid. If it's too stiff, add a little more milk; too liquid, add a little flour. Gently fold in the blueberries, distributing them throughout the mixture.

5 Divide the mixture between the paper cases and bake in the oven for about 20 minutes or until well-risen and golden brown. Test if the muffins are cooked by inserting a fine skewer – it should come out clean. Leave in the muffin tin for a few minutes before cooling on a wire rack.

6 Store the muffins in a cake tin or sealed airtight container. They will keep well for 3–4 days. Or you can freeze them for up to 1 month.

TIP: The longer you beat the butter and sugar, the lighter the muffins will be.

OR YOU CAN TRY THIS...

– Use cranberries or raspberries instead of blueberries.
– Dust the cooked muffins with a little icing (confectioner's) sugar.
– Sprinkle the muffins with a few rolled oats before baking.
– Serve them with a spoonful of creamy Greek yoghurt.

PEANUT BUTTER POWER BARS

MAKES: 8 | PREP: 15 MINUTES | COOK: 25 MINUTES

14g /BAR

115g/4oz (½ cup) butter

115g/4oz (½ cup) crunchy peanut butter

4 tbsp clear honey

2 ripe bananas, mashed

200g/7oz (scant 2 cups) rolled oats

50g/2oz (scant 4 tbsp) vanilla protein powder

100g/3½oz (scant ¾ cup) dried apricots, chopped

25g/1oz (scant ¼ cup) sesame seeds

a good pinch of salt

75g/3oz (scant ½ cup) dark (bittersweet) chocolate chips

These bars are great power snacks, especially if you're feeling fatigued and need to get energized. If possible, always use organic 100 per cent peanut butter with no added sugar.

1 Preheat the oven to 160°C, 325°F, gas mark 3. Lightly butter a 20 x 20cm (8 x 8in) baking tin (pan) and line with baking parchment.

2 Heat the butter, peanut butter and honey in a pan over a low heat until the butter melts.

3 Remove from the heat and stir in the bananas, oats, protein powder, apricots, sesame seeds and salt until you have a sticky mixture. If it's not firm enough, add more oats; if it's too dry, add a little honey. Lastly, stir in the chocolate chips.

4 Spoon the mixture into the prepared tin, pressing it down well with the back of a metal spoon and smoothing the top.

5 Bake in the oven for about 25 minutes until crisp and golden brown. Leave to cool in the tin before cutting into bars. Store in an airtight container for up to 1 week.

OR YOU CAN TRY THIS...

– Try pumpkin, sunflower, linseed or poppy seeds.
– Add a few drops of vanilla extract.
– Substitute raisins, dried cranberries or chopped dates for the apricots.
– Use agave or maple syrup instead of honey.

PROTEIN HIGH-ENERGY BALLS

MAKES: 30 | PREP: 15 MINUTES | CHILL: 1 HOUR

4.5g
/BALL

175g/6oz (¾ cup) peanut butter
90ml/3fl oz (scant ½ cup) clear honey
125g/4½oz (generous 1 cup) rolled oats
50g/2oz (scant 4 tbsp) chocolate protein powder
25g/1oz (¼ cup) flaxseeds or chia seeds
50g/2oz (generous ¼ cup) dark (bittersweet) chocolate chips
100g/3½oz (1 cup) chopped pistachios

These delicious bite-sized snacks will energise you and boost your protein intake. They are surprisingly filling and the perfect solution for when you're feeling peckish.

1 Put the peanut butter and honey in a pan set over a low heat and stir gently until warm and well combined. Alternatively, use a microwave.

2 Remove from the heat and stir in the oats, protein powder, seeds and chocolate chips, distributing them evenly throughout the mixture. If the mixture is too sticky, add some more oats; if it's too dry, add some honey or peanut butter.

3 Divide the mixture into 30 small pieces and, with your hands, roll each one into a ball.

4 Put the chopped pistachios in a shallow dish and roll the balls in the nuts until they are sparsely coated all over.

5 Arrange the balls on a large baking tray (cookie sheet) lined with baking parchment and chill in the fridge for at least 1 hour until set. Place in an airtight container and keep in the fridge for up to 10 days.

OR YOU CAN TRY THIS...
– Roll the balls in chopped almonds or hazelnuts, toasted flaked almonds, seeds or rolled oats.
– Use vanilla or hemp protein powder instead of chocolate.
– Add a little ground cinnamon.
– Use almond or cashew butter instead of peanut butter.

DESSERTS & BAKING

(25-50G PROTEIN)

APRICOT ALMOND CRUMBLE

SERVES: 4-6 | PREP: 15 MINUTES | COOK: 25-30 MINUTES

900g/2lb ripe apricots,
    halved and stoned (pitted)
4 tbsp caster (superfine) sugar
a dash of lemon juice
crème fraîche or vanilla
    ice cream, to serve

FOR THE CRUMBLE:
175g/6oz (¾ cup) chilled
    butter, diced
100g/3½oz (1 cup) plain
    (all-purpose) flour
100g/3½oz (generous
    1 cup) rolled oats
75g/3oz (scant ¾ cup)
    ground almonds
    (almond meal)
100g/3½oz (generous 1¼
    cups) chopped almonds
100g/3½oz (scant ½ cup)
    soft brown sugar
2 tbsp pumpkin seeds
2 tbsp cold water

TIP: You don't
have to make the
crumble by hand.
Instead, briefly blitz
everything together
in a food processor.

Most fruits are not rich in protein, but apricots are higher than most with 1.4g per 100g/3½oz. They're also a good source of vitamins A and C as well as potassium. This crumble is packed with protein-rich almonds, oats and seeds and the portions for 4 people are generous – for 6 people, it works out at 13g protein per serving.

1 Preheat the oven to 180°C, 350°F, gas mark 4.

2 Put the apricots in an ovenproof dish and sprinkle the sugar and lemon juice over the top.

3 Make the crumble: rub the butter into the flour with your fingertips until it resembles coarse breadcrumbs. Stir in the oats, ground and chopped almonds, sugar and pumpkin seeds. Sprinkle with the cold water and give it a stir to create some small sticky clumps.

4 Sprinkle the crumble mixture over the apricots right up to the edge of the dish. Do this lightly and don't press it down.

5 Bake in the oven for 25–30 minutes until the crumble is crisp and golden brown and the fruit is bubbling around the edges.

6 Leave for 5–10 minutes to cool down a little before serving with crème fraîche or vanilla ice cream.

OR YOU CAN TRY THIS...
– Use chopped walnuts or hazelnuts instead of almonds.
– Add some ground ginger or cinnamon to the crumble.
– Use quartered fresh peaches instead of apricots.
– Serve with custard.

BANANA CINNAMON MUFFINS

MAKES: 12 | PREP: 15 MINUTES | COOK: 20-25 MINUTES

7g /MUFFIN

100g/3½oz (generous 1 cup) rolled oats, plus extra for sprinkling
200g/7oz (2 cups) wholewheat flour
1½ tsp baking powder
1 tsp bicarbonate of soda (baking soda)
½ tsp sea salt
1 tsp ground cinnamon
100g/3½oz (½ cup) light brown sugar
4 large ripe bananas, mashed with a fork
2 medium free-range eggs, beaten
60ml/2fl oz (¼ cup) light olive or sunflower oil
2 tbsp milk
100g/3½oz (scant 1 cup) chopped walnuts
4 tbsp sesame seeds
1 tsp demerara sugar

These delicious muffins are full of nutritional goodness and are great for a quick snack or breakfast on the go. What's more, they're really easy to make and they keep well in the fridge for another day.

1 Preheat the oven to 180°C, 350°F, gas mark 4. Line a 12-hole muffin tin (pan) with paper cases (liners).

2 Put the oats, flour, baking powder, bicarbonate of soda, sea salt, cinnamon and light brown sugar in a large bowl. Mix together and make a well in the centre.

3 In another bowl, mix the mashed bananas with the beaten eggs, oil and milk.

4 Stir gently into the oat mixture with the nuts and seeds – don't over-mix. Spoon into the paper cases and sprinkle lightly with the demerara sugar and extra oats.

5 Bake in the oven for 20–25 minutes until golden brown and a skewer inserted in the middle of a muffin comes out clean.

6 Leave to cool, then store in an airtight container in the fridge for up to 4 days.

OR YOU CAN TRY THIS...
– Use chopped pecans or hazelnuts instead of walnuts.
– Flavour with a few drops of vanilla extract.
– Add some dark chocolate chips.

CHOCOLATE PEANUT BUTTER CUPS

MAKES: 12 | PREP: 20 MINUTES | COOK: 5 MINUTES | CHILL/FREEZE: 45-55 MINUTES

7g
/CUP

50g/2oz (¼ cup) icing
    (confectioner's) sugar
25g/1oz (2 tbsp) butter,
    at room temperature
125g/4½oz (½ cup) smooth
    peanut butter
1 tbsp coconut flour
¼ tsp fine sea salt
700g/1lb 9oz (4 cups)
    dark (bittersweet)
    chocolate chips

Home-made peanut butter cups taste so much better than shop-bought ones and they are usually lower in sugar and higher in protein. For the best results use really dark (bitter-sweet) chocolate (minimum 70% cocoa solids).

1 Line a 12-hole muffin tin (pan) with paper cases (liners).

2 Beat the sugar, butter, peanut butter, coconut flour and salt in a food mixer or with a hand-held electric whisk in a bowl until you have a smooth paste. Chill in the fridge or freezer for 15 minutes.

3 Roll it into a long, thick cylinder and slice into 12 discs. Cover and refrigerate while you melt the chocolate.

4 Melt half of the chocolate chips in a microwave or a heatproof bowl suspended over a pan of simmering water. Divide the melted chocolate between the 12 cases to cover the bases evenly. Put the muffin tin in the freezer for 15–20 minutes until the chocolate sets hard.

5 Remove from the freezer and place a peanut butter disc in each case. Melt the remaining chocolate chips and pour over the discs to cover them completely and evenly. Freeze for 15–20 minutes until set.

6 Store the peanut butter cups in a sealed container in the fridge. They will keep well for up to 1 week. Serve them chilled or at room temperature.

OR YOU CAN TRY THIS...
– Use almond or cashew butter instead of peanut butter to make the cups.
– Sprinkle a few sea salt flakes over the melted chocolate before freezing at the end.

FRUITY NUTTY CHOCOLATE BARS

SERVES: 12 | PREP: 15 MINUTES | COOK: 20-30 MINUTES

9.5g
/SERVE

45g/1½oz (generous ¼ cup) ground almonds (almond meal)

300g/10oz (3¼ cups) rolled oats

a pinch of salt

150g/5oz (1 cup) chopped almonds

100g/3½oz (generous ½ cup) dried figs, chopped

100g/3½oz (scant ¾ cup) ready-to-eat dried apricots, chopped

1 tbsp chia seeds

1 tbsp pumpkin seeds

1 tbsp sunflower seeds

1 tbsp sesame seeds

50g/2oz dark (bittersweet) chocolate, chopped

150g/5oz (generous ½ cup) butter, plus extra for greasing

85ml/3fl oz (generous ¼ cup) clear honey

2 tbsp almond butter

These crunchy snack bars are a real treat and give you a protein boost. They keep well for a few days, so bake some at the weekend and you'll have a supply to get you through the week.

1 Preheat the oven to 170°C, 325°F, gas mark 3. Line a buttered 30 x 20cm (12 x 8in) baking tin (pan) with baking parchment.

2 Put the ground almonds, oats, salt, almonds, dried fruit, seeds and chocolate in a bowl and mix together well.

3 Put the butter, honey and almond butter in a pan set over a very low heat and stir gently until the butter melts and everything is well blended. Pour over the dry ingredients and mix well. If it's too dry, add more melted butter; too sticky, add more oats.

4 Transfer the mixture to the prepared tin and level the top. Bake in the oven for 20–30 minutes until golden brown.

5 Remove and leave to cool slightly before cutting into 12 bars. When completely cold, remove from the tin and place in an airtight container. They will stay fresh for up to 5 days.

OR YOU CAN TRY THIS...

– Add cacao nibs or hemp or poppy seeds.
– Flavour with a few drops of vanilla extract.
– Substitute crunchy peanut butter for the almond butter.

PROTEIN PAVLOVA

SERVES: 6 | PREP: 25 MINUTES | COOK: 1–1¼ HOURS

10.5g /SERVE

4 large egg whites
¼ tsp cream of tartar
225g/8oz (generous 1 cup) caster (superfine) sugar
250g/9oz (generous 1 cup) mascarpone
200ml/7fl oz (generous ¾ cup) double (heavy) cream
grated zest and juice of 1 lemon
1 tbsp maple syrup (optional)
3 ripe large peaches, stoned (pitted) and chopped
300g/10oz blackberries
50g/2oz (⅔ cup) toasted flaked almonds

TIP: Instead of cream of tartar you can beat in 2 teaspoons cornflour (cornstarch) and 2 teaspoons white wine vinegar after adding all the sugar.

In this spectacular pavlova, topped with lemony mascarpone cream and fresh fruit, there's protein not only in the egg whites but also in the mascarpone, cream, peaches, blackberries and flaked almonds.

1 Preheat the oven to 140°C, 275°F, gas mark 1. Line a large baking tray (cookie sheet) with baking parchment. Draw a 23cm/9in circle on the paper as a guide.

2 Whisk the egg whites in a food mixer or a large clean bowl until they form soft peaks. Whisk in the cream of tartar and then gradually add the sugar, a tablespoon at a time, beating well between each addition, until the mixture is stiff and really glossy.

3 Spoon the meringue into the circle you've drawn on the baking parchment, spreading it out with a spatula and making a slight hollow in the middle.

4 Place in the oven and immediately lower the temperature to 130°C, 250°F, gas mark ½ and bake for 1–1¼ hours or until crisp on top but still slightly soft inside. Turn off the oven and leave the meringue inside until it is completely cold.

5 Beat together the mascarpone and cream, then beat in the lemon zest and juice until smooth. Beat in the maple syrup (if using).

6 Peel the paper away from the base of the pavlova and place on a serving plate. Spread with the mascarpone cream and top with the peaches, blackberries and toasted flaked almonds. Cut into slices to serve.

OR YOU CAN TRY THIS...
– Flavour the meringue with a few drops of vanilla extract.
– Vary the fruit: try apricots and raspberries or fresh figs, orange segments and pomegranate seeds (arils).
– Use lime zest and juice or vanilla extract to flavour the mascarpone cream.

CHOCOLATE ESPRESSO POTS

SERVES: 4 | PREP: 15 MINUTES | COOK: 5 MINUTES | CHILL: 30 MINUTES

12g /SERVE

150g/5oz dark (bittersweet) chocolate (minimum 70% cocoa solids)
450g/1lb silken tofu, drained
100ml/3½fl oz (generous ⅓ cup) maple syrup
3 tbsp bitter espresso coffee
a few drops of vanilla extract
a pinch of sea salt flakes
25g/1oz (¼ cup) chopped pistachio nuts

TIP: Make sure you drain the tofu well, squeezing out as much liquid as possible.

Who would have thought that a little chocolate pot could give your daily protein intake a boost? But that's just what this recipe does. Tofu is a good source of protein, with 7g per 100g … and these pots are vegan-friendly, too.

1 Break the chocolate into pieces and place in a heatproof bowl suspended over a pan of simmering water. Leave until the chocolate melts, stirring occasionally, then remove from the heat.

2 Blitz the tofu, maple syrup, espresso coffee, vanilla and salt in a blender or food processor until smooth and creamy. Add the melted chocolate and blitz briefly until well mixed and smooth.

3 Divide the mixture between 4 ramekins or glass bowls. Leave in the fridge for at least 30 minutes until set.

4 Sprinkle with the chopped pistachios before serving.

OR YOU CAN TRY THIS...
– Substitute agave syrup for the maple syrup.
– Add a sprinkling of ground cinnamon.
– Decorate with chocolate shavings and coffee beans.
– Top with finely chopped hazelnuts or almonds instead of pistachios.

INDEX

1 3 5 7 9 10 8 6 4 2

Published in 2020 by Ebury Press an imprint of Ebury Publishing,
20 Vauxhall Bridge Road,
London SW1V 2SA

Ebury Press is part of the Penguin Random House group of companies
whose addresses can be found at global.penguinrandomhouse.com

Text © Ebury Press 2020
Design © Ebury Press 2020
Photography © Ebury Press 2020

Heather Thomas has asserted her right to be identified as the author of this Work in accordance
with the Copyright, Designs and Patents Act 1988

Design: Louise Evans
Photography: Joff Lee
Food stylist: Mari Williams
Editor: Sam Crisp

First published by Ebury Press in 2020

www.penguin.co.uk

A CIP catalogue record for this book is available from the British Library

ISBN 9781529106565

Printed and bound in China by C&C Offset Printing Co., Ltd

The information in this book has been compiled by way of general guidance in relation to
the specific subjects addressed, but it is not a substitute and not to be relied on for medical,
healthcare, pharmaceutical or other professional advice on specific circumstances and in specific
locations. Please consult your GP, or a qualified professional, before changing your diet. So far as
the author is aware the information given is correct and up to date as at October 2019. Practice,
laws and regulations all change, and the reader should obtain up to date professional advice on
any such issue. The author and the publishers disclaim, as far as the law allows, any liability arising
directly or indirectly from the use, or misuse, of the information contained in this book.

Penguin Random House is committed to a sustainable future for our business, our readers and our
planet. This book is made from Forest Stewardship Council® certified paper.